THE NOTES AND TONES
OF OUR EVANGELISM
AND OTHER STUDIES

By
ROBERT FERGUSON

LONDON: THE EPWORTH PRESS

To the
METHODIST MINISTERIAL BROTHERHOOD
—and to my Fellow Members of the F.K.—
With deep appreciation of fifty years of
happy fellowship and service
and
with tenderest remembrance of many who " once
were comrades of our way " to whom I owe and own
an incalculable debt amongst whom I number
P. O. H., J. G., J. B. B., J. T., J. R., A. S. P., A. L. H.,
W. L. W., G. B., J. A. C., W. R. M., W. F. H., G. J.,
W. B. B., A. H., D. A., J. A. A., W. G., W. B., A. T.,
C. L. S., J. B., R. R., J. A. M., G. L. P., J. E. N., F. H.,
M. F., S. J. J., A. J. W., H. D., J. P., and H.S.

SURELY THEY ARE AMONG
" THE HORSEMEN AND CHARIOTS ROUND ABOUT "
WHO HELP US FROM " WITHIN THE VEIL."

FOREWORD

BY THE CHAIRMAN
OF THE SCOTLAND DISTRICT
REV. CECIL D. EADES

ONE of the high privileges of serving the Methodist Church in Scotland is to share in the unique fellowship which binds our ministers together North of the Border.

Perhaps geography and the smallness of our numbers make us turn to one another with great eagerness, but no one has paid a greater contribution to our happy unity than our beloved brother the Rev. Robert Ferguson.

Although in the fiftieth year of his ministry, in mind and spirit and keenness he is one of the youngest men among us. Time and again we have shared in his practical generosity, but also in the richness of his mind and spirit.

We have received so much from him in our Glasgow Fraternal and Scottish Ministerial Retreats that a number of us have urged Mr Ferguson to put some of these treasures which have enriched us into more permanent form.

Although very widely read, everything has to pass through the crucible of Mr Ferguson's original and incisive mind.

In short, he is a man who thinks for himself, and his expressions and emphases are unique.

To hear our Brother and see his radiant face as he speaks is a benediction, but I for one am devoutly thankful to have the opportunity of pondering frequently on the mature reflections of this humble man of prayer and prophetic insight.

CECIL D. EADES.

PREFACE

IT seemed to me that, as my fifty years of ministry coincided with the year of Evangelism planned by our World Methodist Church, I might be able to render a simple service to a great cause, and at the same time celebrate a personal event.

What I am able to do is but to put in a footnote to what is being so admirably done by our Home Missionary Department and many others.

With these little studies I combine my earnest prayer that 1953 may be " the acceptable Year of the Lord " for our whole world Church.

My brethren have been all too kind in their appreciation of that part of these studies which they have heard in speech, and I would never have ventured to print them had they not re-assured me of their welcome.

My mind chimes to Baron von Hugel's sentiments when he said that he was anxious that nothing he wrote should be " pushed," but that such poor things should drop down like seed and produce fruit if the God who was so kind to birds and seeds found He could bless them in any degree.

I am deeply indebted to our " Great Heart " of a Chairman for his all too generous Foreword.

It is the greatest joy conceivable to work together under his benevolent and gifted leadership.

I am pleased to be able to send this little book to the students in our Colleges as well as to our fellow ministers, for I think these studies may have an additional value to those who are " girding on the armour."

I had thought right up to a late moment of sending out this book under the nom-de-plume of " Anglo-Scot," so that no one would feel there was any obligation to acknowledge it, but my friends pressed me not to use a pen-name, and I have, a little reluctantly, yielded to this wish.

It gives an added pleasure to date these studies as " Xmas," seeing that was our Scottish mother's birthday, and we as a family love to celebrate the mercy of God which gave us such a mother.

ROBERT FERGUSON.

KIRKCALDY
Christmas 1952

CONTENTS

The Notes and Tones of Our Evangelism

I WOULD like, if I may, to use three similes, which will enable me to make my plea, and press a conviction I have long held.

(1) A piece of cat-gut tightly strung and smartly struck will emit a note, but it requires that cat-gut to be stretched on the sensitive fibres of a violin or 'cello to emit a tone. (2) A note sounded from a conductor's tuning fork is a good lead, but it remains thin and tenuous, and dies on the air unless taken up by the singers in chords and in chorus. (3) A musical theme or motif after the grand manner is incomplete in itself; it calls for instrumentation and orchestration and needs to be inter-woven in endless variations and combinations before its potential beauty and glory can be expressed.

And our Gospel in its announcement and heralding is but a note; basic indeed, and indispensable, but however powerfully we strike it as a *note*, it has little challenge in it or carrying power unless it is *toned* in the personal life of the preacher who under-takes to be its witness. Our Gospel note, too, is a " lead " which calls for a Christian community to pick up, accompany and amplify. *The* Gospel is *our* Gospel, as well as *my* Gospel; and the full chords and chorus accompaniment are an integral part of its full rendering.

In the Gospel, too, there is what Dr. Forsyth called " the grand manner." In it there is the central pulse of God's loving heart and of His great initiative for the reconciliation of all things to Himself. And a theme of such sweep and scope must be progressively interwoven into every relationship of life and sound itself in ever varying ways throughout the ever changing forms of the complex life of man. Only so can the Divine motif to " sum up all things in Christ " be brought to its fullest expression and climax.

Where Our Gospel "Lives."—Charles Kingsley in his Eversley Vicarage, we are told, would sometimes ask his boys to hand him down a book from the shelves, and turning over its pages would say, " I want to show you where it *lives*."

I suppose it is true to say that in general, things live when they combine and blend; become integrated. When, too, things which have a pre-ordained affinity for each other come together, there results a certain " newness of life." Biologically, things mated become creative, and on the level of personal life an individual finds his richer life in the blendings of fellowship. When the material and the imponderable come together as they do in the magnetic needle and the dynamo, you get what is " live." When two worlds come together in the overture and response of Christian living, the spirit of man experiences what is both sacramental and " live."

And surely it is when the Christian Gospel gets its resonances from the receiving heart and the sensitive mind and the active service and sympathy of the believing man, that it takes on a reinforced and irresistible life. The good news finds its true nuance in the good life and the goodly fellowship. The buoyancy of the believing heart and the jubilant fellowship of the Christan community sends out reverberations which compel attention, and break into a world full of noises with an enchanting music all its own.

I suppose the scholars would put it in this wise : The *Kerygma* —the preaching—has its life in the *Koinonia*—the fellowship. They live in and through each other. The herald stands inside his message as a witness, and the whole Christian fellowship life is the sensitive fibre which tones the truth he proclaims and makes it " live " and bears it on."

Our declarations of the Gospel need the accompaniment of demonstrations to get across. The doctrines of our Gospel are but the carbon filament—the instrumental means by which what is " live " manifests itself.

" Where's the Lag ? "—The pressing question which lies heavily on the Christian heart is " *Where's the lag ?* "

In two stories in the Old Testament and the New which tell of ineffectual attempts at miracle working—that of Gehazi using the prophet's staff to awaken the Shunammite's child, and the failure of the nine disciples to expel an evil spirit in the absence of their Lord—the lag was the absence of accompaniments ; in the one case of a prophetic personality and in the other of a spirit of prayer. There was in both cases the presence of an acute problem and the material and personal instruments of effectiveness, but the failure lay in the inability to incorporate them with the "imponderables." The instruments were there, but they were not implemented. They remained in isolation. There was the reiterative without the creative. There was the paraphernalia without the power.

It would seem as if in all the wide range of life, isolation consorts with inertia and force is allied with integration. The babe is still-born if the conjunction is lacking between the oxygen of the air and the child's potential lung. So many things in our Christian faith and message are sublimely complementary one of the other and, the lag lies so often in our slipping up on the other foot—at one time the right foot, at others the left.

The ancient exclamation of the prophet seems relevant to our situation "Thy tacklings are loosed," and as a consequence we can neither "stengthen our mast" nor "spread our sail." Our doctrines and declarations lie too loosely tied up with our common life, and it is difficult to fulfil the call of the World Church to "set up signs that all the world can see" so long as the mast is aslant and tottering, and our sails too insecurely fastened to be given the full play of all the winds of God.

A Rationale of Evangelism.—Though the purpose of this study is intensely practical, it may not be without value to try to form, even crudely, a rationale of evangelism. Ought it, I wonder, to run something like this ?

In any living Universe " nature will out." Life will disclose itself and fulfil itself in its expressions. In a world with a mind of its own—which is what we mean by believing in God—what is purposive in that mind will seek embodiment in what is congruous with itself. In our Christian faith our starting point and key-note is the mind of Christ ; and that mind was essentially a Gospel mind. Grace and Truth came by Jesus Christ. The truth as it is in Jesus is fundamentally evangelical, and no expression of that truth is congruous, which is not redemptively red and lovingly rescuing. That is the Conductor's tuning fork which awakens all the chords of Gospel music and dictates the theme of all succeeding combinations. The opening bars and the second—and twenty-second—movement must be in alignment and be an amplification of the original theme. The tone must reinforce the note and be in accord with it.

B

And as " the truth as it is in Jesus " is truth integrated with life ; and incarnated there ; and as that truth is as much or more in deed than in word, there must be an interpretation of that truth in terms of life, and in terms of personal relationship ; and in and through all, interpretation must move step by step with integration and the whole lead to a mediation of that truth in personal and communal action.

What is this Grace and Truth ?—We easily " slip up " if we fail to distinguish between the various orders of truth and their true cognates.   Truth, of an academic or speculative order, finds its adequate expression in coherence.   The mind cannot rest in incoherence, and this order of truth must compose the passion of man to hold things together, and harmoniously. Scientific truth is more directly constrained in the interests of practical living, and in applied science it has its fullest justification and fulfilment.   Religious truth—and supremely—Christian truth—has a personal and existential character.   Its orbit is not impersonal, and its world cannot be characterised as " it." It is an entrance upon an " I and Thou " relationship in which a personal encounter is involved and in which we are under an obligation to take up an attitude and to decide.

And truth in this realm, as it brings its bestowment and succour, makes at the same time its demand.   The relationships of overture and response are involved.   And the response to be made is to chime with this kind of truth's keynote which is truth out to rescue and reconcile.

And Grace is Love on the gradient, out to relieve and recover. It cannot remain outside human need and sorrow and sin.   It must identify itself with the life and lot of those it would rescue and save.

And it is not too much to say that both Grace and Truth are careering things—active, seeking, saving impulses of the heart of God beating in the Saviour's ministry from beginning to end.   They represent the nature of God which will " out," which cannot be constrained but must move swiftly to our relief.   As careering things they ask of us " free course " that they may " run and be glorified."   They call for mediation by their very nature.

The Principle of Congruity Comes In.—The principle of congruity must always be a constituent of any rationale of evangelism. Things must chime and be in accord with one another. It comes in as a criterion in all life—in dress, in decoration, in landscape, in music—indeed everywhere !

In philosophy, too, congruity is a determinative and constituent element by whatever name the system of thought is known. It receives, too, its rightful place of honour in Holy Writ. Solomon's plea that the temple he was to erect was to be exceeding magnifical, rested on the ground that " The house that is to be builded . . . must be great, for great is our God." The Psalmist too exclaims that " Great is the Lord and greatly to be praised." In honour of the same principle, our Lord's own imperative impulses expressed in His " musts " surely rested back on what was sublimely congruous to His mind and mission. The writer in the Epistle to the Hebrews stresses, as did our Lord in His word on the way to Emmaus, what " it behoved " Christ to do and suffer. Throughout the New Testament, too, when Apostles declare that " necessity is laid upon them to preach," that they " cannot but speak the things they do see and hear," that " the love of Christ constrains them "—we get abundant evidence that our Christian faith is only " in character " and congruous with its original impulse when it is evangelising. This is the heart pulse in it all.

The waters which are precipitated down the Lough Rigg and the Scarsdale Pike find their channel to Morecombe Bay and the Irish Sea by way of Rydal Water and Grasmere and Windermere and the River Leven, but the one pulse beats in all—the pulse received from its head-waters, and original fountain. So the pulses of evangelistic action all lie back in the very nature of Redeeming Love which must " out."

Beauty of Tone.—The essential nature of our Gospel is always determinative and decisive as to the character of its mediums and manifestations. Being fully personal itself, it demands what is personal in ourselves as the indispensable unit of its expressions and outworkings.

And being the overflowing of God's own life into the realm of time and the sphere of human experience of what the New Testament calls " His fulness," the only human response which is really in character is in what is total. And here, totalitarian concepts and categories are relevant as nowhere else.

This life of the Gospel, however, because it is so personal, takes on distinctiveness through the human instrument which mediates it. Individuals vary in the texture and constitution of their thought and feeling as much as any stringed instrument, like the violin or 'cello do. And the touch of the living medium is always a considerable factor in the discoursing of the same musical composition. Paganini's violin and Kriesler's touch were both elements in the marvel of their music.

The father of Matilde Verne—as she tells us in her *Chords of Remembrance*—had a mania for buying violins, and would try them out on the family and get their judgment on their differences. Matilde herself, when a pupil of Madame Clara Schumann, at first disappointed her teacher by contenting herself with mere correctness in her fingering, only to discover at length that the Madame's sensitive spirit was listening for beauty of tone as well. The technique was not at fault, but delicacy of touch was wanting—as indeed it often is in our own discoursing of our Gospel theme.

Gospel Unity in Diversity.—It follows then, that the Gospel is always the same and yet is never " in character " if there is a kind of neutral sameness in it. The Gospel—like God Himself—both universalises its manifestations and individuates them. The wide ranges of the truth as it is in Jesus are complemented by the wide ranges and differences which make up human personalities. Such differences run through the whole piece and texture of each one of us. The elements are never mixed equally in even the closest friends. The variations are represented in our visual and tactile mindedness, right down to the artistic or non-artistic formation of our fingers. Our temperamental differences are often as opposite as the poles. Whilst we are all bound together in the bundle of life, we are as variously shaped individually as any bundle of firewood sticks. Not only do some of us get our knowledge pictorially while others get it audibly, but some of us think more closely in our feeling and only think clearly when we feel deeply ; whereas others have a time-lag between thinking and feeling, and thinking only slowly precipitates into the emotional texture of their life.

Those who have been under the ministry of those two intimate friends Alex Whyte and Marcus Dods will readily recognise how those differences were strongly marked in them. Their custom was to take a walk together on a Saturday afternoon to Arthur's Seat, and the mind and heart of both chimed to the central truth of the Gospel. But hear them next morning !

Alex Whyte's whole features and bearing mediated the thought and warmth of the Gospel; exhaled it with the quality of a richly emotional soul, superadded. Marcus Dods, with an equally Gospel-minded loyalty, mediated the truth without seeming emotion, along the level track of a reasoned discourse in a voice which seldom softened and with a face which was rarely modified in feeling.

The Range of Gospel Truth.—There are variations, too, in the content and context of Gospel truth which call for variation in the interpretation and mediation of it. Some men are better fitted to represent one aspect of it than another, though all are on their honour to see and communicate it as a whole to the utmost of their power. Professor Du Bose used to say that he regarded it as one of his chief tasks to endeavour to see that aspect of truth which he was most prone to ignore. Our ministries in retrospect furnish many of us with plenty of evidence that we may have failed just there. Paul was justified as none of us are, in claiming that he had kept back nothing either of himself or of the whole counsel of God, in his testifying to the grace of God.

One may not be far from the facts in saying that Grace represents the curves and Truth the straight lines of the Gospel. John Oman in his *Grace and Personality* pleads that Grace cannot take its way like an arrow to its mark, but must in order to safeguard the freedom of the personality it would rescue, make its curving course round about human obduracy and resistance. Truth, however, is not a thing which yields. Like Amos' plumbline, it must disclose what is out of the straight, and never bend its measuring line. The two are not contraries, but in some aspects are opposites and complementaries.

John Wesley was careful throughout his whole ministry to keep the Law and Gospel in fertilising touch with each other. In the Gospel we are disburdened of the Law, but never disown it. From being fulfilled in a servile temper, we come to fulfil it in a filial. Which takes the foreground and which the background, the situation must decide. All Law makes our preaching arid. All Gospel, in its narrower sense, would make our preaching vaporous.

The story of the Southern merchant who came to Scotland and heard three preachers is pertinent here. One, a majestic looking man, preached God's Law; another, Samuel Rutherford, spoke meltingly of God's Love; the other, David Dickson of Irvine, showed him all his heart. Every varied aspect of the truth, at fitting times, calls for mediation from us all.

Gospel Truth Toned in Personal Life.—Living wholes have their pulses in all their parts, and it is often discussed whether those pulses have their priority in the mind or in the heart. These pulses, in most of us are strongest in the heart. If, of course, we think of the heart as the Hebrews did, there is no ground for debate at all. Sir James Mackenzie used to say that the pulses in the various ventricles of the heart were seldom uniform; a strong beat might be in one ventricle and a much feebler one in another. A feeble pulse like that of the Mediterranean might be in one and a stronger pulse like that of the Atlantic in another. Bergson set out to claim—convincingly one thinks—that we circuit life and truth in our thinking, merely discoursing about it, while we take a direct plunge into it in our intuitional and emotional life. Our thought—life—it would appear—whilst existing as an integral part of our personal texture, is seldom in the lead. Life is always prior to thought, and is a fuller, richer, warmer element than it.

However, in the deep mystery of our being, there is no doubt that thought is always accompanied by its penumbra of feeling and is never an isolated element. Moreover, a process of fertilising one part of our nature by another is continually being exercised. Thought pollenates feeling, and feeling thought, and a flowering in the mind and heart result. In the assimilative and associative operations of the total life the great things are begotten, and in and through them all there works the great Spirit of God, mystically uniting the various activities of the whole person, and seeking to make them fruitful in living word and deed.

Communion with the Truth.—Truth, by its nature, calls for attention and appreciation as one of its prior requirements. Dean Inge has a sentence I have remembered throughout my ministry : " No truth, however patent, is ever real to us except as we give it our attention " Truth seeps into our mind as we brood over it, percolating into the very stuff of living. John Denholm Brash had a card in his study, if I remember rightly, bearing the words of Coleridge, " Communion with the truth gives it power over us. The deliverance of the truth after long

communion with it gives it an invincible power over others."
What we speak of as "weight" in a man's utterance of the
Gospel is due to this communion. Apart from it the most vital
things will seem lightweights. Moody used to walk by the
Connecticut river, letting—as he said—"the truth soak in."

Sir Walter Raleigh, whether the first one or the second I am
not quite sure, expressed himself in disparagement of those who
"had no ownership in their facts," who do not incorporate
them in any way with themselves ; who live apart from them.
And Gospel truth above all must be minted in the mind and
mated in the heart. Memorising of it may help, but the deeper
process of appropriation must follow. Luther's insistence that
the personal pronouns contain the very heart of the Gospel is
applicable here, as is also the word of a very different type of
man, John Stuart Mill, who affirmed that "Half the errors
which afflict our race are due to the fact that men cease to think
and ponder those truths which are no longer the subject of
debate." And seeing this page is almost made up of quotations,
another may be added to match the first, of Dean Inge too :
"What we take for granted we do not take at all."

The Interpretation of Truth.—The interpretation of truth
follows in true sequence from communion with it. Interpretation
of its vital meaning to ourselves is of freshening and fertilising
value. To give ideas a framework of words stamps their image
on our minds. Life's double process of "getting our outs in"
and "getting our ins out" are both facilitated by the coinage
of truth in words—formulating the things we want to know and
want to tell. The little girl's reply to her mother has much
hidden wisdom in it : "How can I know what I think till I see
what I say." Mr Asquith, I think, said of Lloyd George, that
"he thought at the tip of his tongue." Others think at the
point of their pen. But whether one or the other, the endeavour
is to give form to what might only exist as vapour, and to
crystallise what would otherwise remain as an unrelated mass.
Dr. Fosdick speaks of the two processes of the mind which are
complementary, the turning of batter into crust and the reverse
process of turning crust back again into batter.

When the interpretations of Gospel truth have to be made to
others, another context than that of our mind has to be kept in
view. We cannot transfer our experience of the truth, but must
transcribe it to men. The ancients' problem is also our modern

one, as it is that of every age : " The preacher sought to find acceptable words, words which like a goad probe, and which like nails reinforce. To know our Gospel is one thing, and supremely important : to know that men stand in need of it, that the truth as it is in Jesus meets need as it is in life, is superlatively important too," but to find an " Interpreter, one among a thousand," to get the truth across intelligibly, is tremendously important as well, though in the mercy of God, " where there's a will there's a way."

The Integration of Truth with Life.

—The integration of Gospel truth with life is the prior condition of any effective interpretation and proclamation of it. Truth such as this, with purposiveness in it, must not only suffuse our thought but spill over into life and action. When Florence Nightingale was brooding over how God wanted her to answer His call, and her friends urged her to express herself in writing, she felt that such an evasion would grieve the Holy Spirit, for, she said, " I think such high feelings only waste themselves in words." No true wholeness of personality is possible if, as with Amiel, our appreciation ends in something less than action and witness. General Smuts pleads in his *Holism* that it would help many to the discovery of the spiritual kernal of personality if those with a real inner life of integration would make frequent and faithful record and witness of it. Certainly, our own greatest enrichments and inspirations have come from fellowship with such lives ; lives like that of Irene Petrie's, which gave the impression of being " utterly satisfied " since life had brought them its supreme gift of serenity. We should all agree, too, with the poor girl in one of Dickens's stories who, having come to know a gracious lady of this Order, exclaimed, " If there were more o' the likes o' you, there'd be fewer o' the likes o' us, there would, there would."

It is in this order of our Christian witness where " the trumpet gives the uncertain sound," and where those who have their place among the uninstructed are unable to say " Amen." All they perceive about us is our babble, and the tongue in which we express our Christian faith is an unknown tongue to them. With a fuller integration of our Christian truth with life and action they would be constrained to fall down on their faces worshipping God and declaring that God is in you of a truth.

The Resulting Mediation.—Mediation is a resultant, the crown and climax of all else. In early Church history, as recorded in the Acts, as we catch the refrain " so mightily grew the Word of God and prevailed," it is significant how closely associated this growth is with some outstanding instance of action in witness and mediation. How impressive it would be if we could get some interlinear history of the progress of the Gospel in both its earlier and later days. I feel sure we should discover the Gospel beating anew, in every instance, in the fountain of its first beginnings. For always there is more than meets the eye or reaches the ear in this glorious story. The account would include Paul's delivery, not of the Gospel only, but " our own souls also " : the same Apostle's willingness to be poured out as a libation over the sacrifice in the service of the Faith. It would include our own honoured Father's eyes filled with tears, His heart with love, and His mouth with arguments as He offered Christ to men. It might, too, have as an addendum little Dinah Morris's question after hearing the good man's sermon on " The Spirit of the Lord is upon me "—" Auntie, will he go back to heaven to-night after the preaching? "—and how much else. Mediation like a stream cuts its own channels and follows its own law in its pulsings.

When that gracious lady, Madame Clara Schumann, played her husband's music in Vienna after his passing, the audience rose in acclaim and cried, " Schumann is alive ! " He was alive in his wife's mediation of him. And what were the factors which made such a conveyance possible ? There was her intimate communion with his spirit, there was the additional aid of his photograph on the piano as she played, and there was over and above her gifted technique, the reading of his love-letters before the performance. And all reached their realisation in the overt act by which she joined in mystic union the material instrument with the imponderable inspirational spring.

Which things are an allegory.

Evangelism in its Second Context, in the Church.—Evangelism's second context, is as indispensable and fundamental as the first. As the hand is only a hand when incorporated in the body and is only fully itself then, so the Gospel is only the Gospel when the Church's life lies behind it and within it. No one can fail to observe that when the Apostolic note was sounded, it was taken up " together " in the corporate life of the

Church. Indeed, everything was " together "—worship, witness, breaking of bread, and prayer. It would be true to say that Evangelism's unit was plural as much as it was singular : the two or three were as much the base as the one. When new converts were added it was equally " to the Lord " and " to the Church." And the " added " was not like the addition of stones to a heap harmonising with some physical law of gravity, but like the addition of leafage and fruitage to a tree, the presence and potential of which had been there from the beginning by the very law of organic life. The individual and the corporate fit into each other, as Peter tries to say by that strain of symbolism which he adopts—" As living stones we are built up as a spiritual house." And Paul, using the same symbolism, says, " As a holy temple in the Lord." We, too, with the free use of symbolism, may say that the individual and corporate factors in the Church's life, are fitly framed into each other, stabilise each other, and also freshen and fertilise each other's life.

Together they share newness of life, together they take the lead given to them by the Apostolic note, and together they sound it out that all the world may hear.

And our Lord makes His richest promises to us as we meet together and agree together. Different as we are—as different as the parts taken by the soprano and the bass—as answering the one Conductor's baton we cordially agree in the glorious music that we render.

Evangelism in its Third Context.—As I brooded over this third and wider context wherein we are to sound the Apostolic note together—leaving mind and heart open to other impulses than my own—I opened the morning paper and discovered that Sir Hugh Roberton, the Orpheus Choir conductor, had passed on. How some of us remember his trim, lithe figure as he swayed his sinuous hands to bring in the several parts of his chorus, always himself so unusually taking part in the singing as though joy did make him sing. One thought, too, of what lay behind the public performance, the endless rehearsing, the unceasing drilling to bring tempo and tone into full alignment with the theme. How, too, average singers through their training and by their combination were raised to magical heights in the transmission of their musical imponderables.

It was always evident that the spirit of one had passed into the many. What was not quite so evident—as Sir Hugh himself confessed—the spirit of the many passed into the one. The Choir and he grew together. There was a mystic interplay which defied all analysis. The Conductor himself averred that what he passed on had been passed on to him by the blithe and merry little woman who was his mother. He stepped into the world with a song on his lips and " he sent it on." He had nothing he had not received.

All of which presents, colourfully and musically, that (1) We pass on what we have first received—everything rests on the " given "; (2) That behind all our public presentation of Gospel truth there must be the intimacies and drilling of study, fellowship, and prayer, the rehearsing which brings us together into the alignment of tone and tempo in Gospel truth; (3) And then—those who overhear and are listening to this choral music are lifted too, so that, as always happened at an Orpheus Concert, the whole audience ended by singing as an Augmented Choir.

The Evangel and Our Accompaniment of It.—We would, I fear, have to agree that the music capable of setting the whole world singing is not getting its merited accompaniment from any of us. A way out must be found, as John Wesley found it a couple of centuries ago.

A musical critic in his obituary notice of Sir Hugh Roberton said, " He answered the urge which led him to lift choral singing out of the dull rut and set it soaring." And surely that is precisely what our Methodist Founder did, on another level. He was taken from the dead centre of his own works and was led by the Spirit to rest on " the given." And " the given," he saw, was to be " given away." It must be transmitted. So he drew round him groups of men and women far below the average, and by the drilling and moulding influence of the Society Class he got them to chime together. By each and every one of them playing their part, the world around caught the music, and were led in ones and twos, and tens, and dozens, to listen in and then join in swelling the song. The Church of England of that day seemed content to sound the note, but here was the veritable tone. And that tone had a choral enrichment and expansion in an infinite number of ways. The choral rendering of the Gospel was veritably lifted out of the dull rut. And just as there is no defence against a fragrance, there was no defence against enchanting song which met you everywhere. Syren music had its bewitching lure broken by this new Orpheus.

What Butler's lofty note in itself could not do for the freeing of Britain's soul, this music of the Gospel did.

And ours it is to give a new choral rendering of this Gospel music—this Passion Chorale, this Hallelujah Chorus. For ours it is, in Dr. Dennye's memorable words—not to produce irrefragable arguments but to produce irresistible impressions. So

> " The Song in them, in us, is one—
> We raise it high, we send it on
> The Song that never endeth."

A Wider Context Yet.—But Evangelism has a wider context yet. The Recitative of the first Christmas music was but a prelude to the multitude of the heavenly host praising God. The first singer was the leader of a chorus which sent its echoes resounding everywhere.

> " The beam that shines from Zion's hill
> Shall lighten every land ;
> The King who reigns in Salem's towers,
> Shall all the world command."

It is this sense of a world context which has often been forgotten. What gives Communism no small part of its thrall is that men pick up in it the swing and sweep of a universal movement which brings everything within its compass. Men move to what they believe to be " the music of the spheres." In a sermon I heard yesterday by the Rev. Murdo Macdonald of St. George's West, Edinburgh, this very point was stressed :

(1) Communists see that human nature demands a dynamic creed. (2) They see that human nature demands a revolutionary change. (3) They see that human nature demands a total committal.

And only as our message has that sweep and scope will the children of light show that they are as wise as the children of this world.

Surely we have our Red Flag music as well as they. And there is more red in it than theirs, even as there is more lilt in our music than in theirs. Reality is red and rhythmic for them but on a lower level than ours. And our song is capable of drowning all music but its own.

In Wagner's composition, the pilgrim music is always challenged and almost silenced by the music of the revel. But, in the end, it is the pilgrim music that holds the field. And if our music is of the genuine pilgrim order, there will sound through it the music of the skies, and this in its turn and in its time will conquer all.

The Unfinished Symphony.—The Symphony will always be in the order of time an unfinished symphony, but its music is destined to swell and grow, subduing all things to itself. I used to tell in our celebrations of the Jubilee in my last Church how we decided to have the wire netting taken from the windows and the dirt of years cleared away. Arranging to meet the window cleaner one morning at ten o'clock, I found him busy cleaning the windows of another church in the same street. When at length he got busy with the windows he had engaged to clean, I saw him descend from the ladder frequently to take up some mixture which he applied to the panes. Being curious, I asked what the preparation was, and I was surprised to be told it was " dirt." It set my mind working on how there was One able to subdue all things to Himself. Industry and Commerce and Diplomacy are sometimes traduced by being called " dirt." But there is One who can subdue all these things to His service.

We all know, more or less, how often—to change the figure— Social Life, and Sport, and many another realm of human activity tend to bring in a little tune of their own, which is far from this higher kind of music. Symphony does not rightly describe much of our ordered—or disordered—life with one another. The Kingdom of God, which is the kingdom of right relationships, is not sought first, in the life of society around us. And the unrest of our time is caused far less by economic conditions—though these are never to be underrated or ignored— than by the restless discontent of hearts made to answer to the loftier music of the skies.

In Daniel Niles' words, we are called to " besiege all the ways of life on behalf of Christ." Nothing is to be left out, for what is unsubdued to Christ's sovereignty not only leaves a void, but creates a menace and a complex which has far-reaching repercussions not only in its own sphere, but in all others.

The Church Finds Herself in Her Mission.—It is in the unremitting pursuit of her evangelistic task—without demur and without delay—that the Church of Christ will find herself.

In Kipling's story of the *Diambula*—the ship that found herself—it is claimed that a ship is never a unity when merely held together as rivets and plates can hold it. It only becomes itself when out on the open sea, with the waters washing over her decks and the winds straining her masts and the smoke blackening her funnels, as it takes its appointed way in the great waters to her distant port.

And will not the real Church unity be found in that fashion? This is no disparagement of all that can be done by ecclesiastic joiners and platers and plank-layers. But we can easily expect too much of what may be done in the holding of Conferences, as those appointed to them would be the first to acknowledge.

Just as all political action must needs rest back on an educated public opinion, so all ecclesiastical endeavour after unity must needs be conditioned by the adventurous evangelical passion behind all. A Church must be conceived, not in static categories as something in the dry dock, but as a going concern. It is as we go out on our proper mission we shall find ourselves and find one another and our Lord. Thirty years ago I remember a leader in the Scottish Churches pressed the view that " A Church out to save itself will never save the world, but a Church out to save the world will always save itself."

A literary critic used to tell how difficult he found it to get into the metre of Scott's Marmion. But one day he recited it to himself when on horseback, and found he picked up its rhythm. Later, he discovered that Sir Walter had composed the poem while riding over the sands at Portobello as a Cavalry Officer. And we in our Evangel, as we present it to men, may pick up the very movement of reconciling grace in the heart of God, and as we move with Him, we shall find ourselves and others.

The Significance of Tone.—It may be well at this stage to retrace our steps a little to consider again our main proposition of the significance of tone in our Christian life and witness.

It is a universal language, everybody's mother tongue. It has idioms of its own which require no artifice in translation. The lowliest know it unfailingly for what it is. Like a smile or a fragrance, it carries its own passport and pays no customs dues. It owes and owns no deference to boundary lines and frontiers. It is characterised, too, by an immediacy which admits of no counterfeit. It is the truest exhalation and quintessence of the human spirit. If the level below our conscious life is the fullest total of our being, as can be justifiably claimed, then our tone rather than our talk is our being's sum. It is sincerity's natural and normal medium of expression and the most infallible mediator of the great imponderables of truth. It is insinuating, too, in its processes of communication. It " gets you " before you have time to set up any defences. It influences you well ahead of your consciousness of being influenced at all. It seeps into one unknowingly like the saturations of a mist. There is direct action in it, too, without any warnings or flag wavings.

And being all these things, it is the most potent means the Gospel has for its transmission. There is in it no disdain of intelligible words, but they are its medium and ready instrument and it gives to them its mystic plus.

Development of tone is unconsciously proceeding in us each. Our deep communings with the truth and our committal to it, leave their rich deposits there, as also do our finer or coarser reactions to all life brings. And as sorrow never comes to us unaccompanied, our assimilations of the mystic nutriments of suffering have all their record there.

And supremely, the Spirit of God, the dweller in the innermost, whose operations are so conspicuously in the unutterable, makes His unmistakable contribution there.

Examples of Difference in Tone.—I recall how early in my middle teens Frank Crossley of Ancoats, made a deep impression on our minds as to the supreme importance of tone. He told how he had been personally interested in a case of law, and how the evidence given in a lower court orally, by witnesses, was afterwards read by an opposing counsel in a higher court, and so read as to convey an entirely different impression. And it was the tone did it ; there was no mishandling of words. He reminded us, too, how a household pet, cat or dog, is responsive to tones rather than to words ; how " Go " in the tone of " Come " will bring them to you, and " Come " in the tone of " Go " will send them away.

Dora Greenwell tells how a little maid of hers of simple mind said to her one day, " Miss Greenwell, is the Bible the same in your house as it is in Mr Cornell's, because it sounds different when you read it." It is just the difference of tone.

I used to try to find touch with outsiders in the open air by saying that the Gospel asked something of those of us who spoke it, as well as something from those of us who heard it. And I told a story my father used to tell of a poor and illiterate father and daughter whose runaway and rascally son had sent them a letter which neither of them could read. They first took it to a gruff old butcher who lived nearby, and he read in harsh and rasping tones, " Dear Father, I am very ill, send me some money. Your son, Tom." The old man's spirit kindled with wrath as he heard it read and he burst out, " The scoundrel : not sending us a scrape of a pen for a year and now asking for money. He shan't have a penny." The gentle daughter, however, suggested that they should get the letter read by the kind-hearted grocer, and when in tender tones he read the same words, the old man said, " Poor laddie, he must be very ill to write like that. What can we send him ? "

Tones, a Diversity in Unity.—Like so many things in life, tones represent a diversity in their unity. We can first consider tones as wholes, and then see what diverse elements they combine. Tones are a mystic harmony in a real and inseparable unity.

On the physical level, voice production involves the interplay of difference in the expansive and contractive action of the vocal chords. The heart in its beating has the double action of release and restraint, and there is a corresponding dual action in the inbreathing and outbreathing operation of the lungs.

In all forms of athletic action—in batsmanship and bowling in cricket, as in running, there is the co-ordination of opposites in muscular interplay. And so with tones. What is communicated in the tone of our personal presentation of the Gospel is the total impression made on our spirits by our communings with the grace and truth which are in Christ. Our tone goes flat, if the otherness and holiness of God imminent in the Gospel have given no deep soundings in our experience. On the other hand, our tone is sharp and shrill if the softening and subduing kinsman-redeeming love of Christ has failed to permeate our souls.

All our evaluations of truth are unconsciously evidencing themselves in our witness. When doctrinal formulations are thrust forth, our tone hardens and we give the impression of something we think in, rather than something we live in. When there is a hold-up in the range of our thought or in the obedience of our life, there is impairment in our transmission. The verbal is never a substitute for the vital. To orate the Gospel is not to deliver it : to mouth it is not mediation. Our tones as wholes are always giving us away, and it is tragic when we " give away " the Gospel in the worse sense rather than in the better sense of that phrase.

Tones in their Diversity.—Such considerations of wholeness need not, however, prevent us from considering tones in their diversity. When psychologists treat of our instinctive urges, they differ considerably in their namings and groupings. And we may expect to find similar differences when we speak separately of the tones of our evangelism. There is considerable advantage in definiteness in detailing them, remembering always that they are part of one organic whole. I have long felt the attraction of the figure used by Dr. Michael in his *Commentary on the Philippians*, of the Apostle checking off on his fingers, as if differentiating and then totalling the things he counted loss for Christ, " Circumcised the eighth day. . . ." It seems to fit so splendidly with the irrepressible character of the man. And I see him doing the same thing as he proceeds later with " Whatsoever things are true. . . ."

At the same time, the figure helps us to remember that the things surrendered and the virtues espoused were not made piecemeal, but as a whole, like the opening of the whole hand. We may do the same thing in respect of Evangelism's tone, if we bear in mind the same proviso.

And then, as there are different combinations of the fingers in different actions of the hand, so we may the more readily see how these notes seem so readily to combine with each other. They seem to pair off, balancing and modifying one another, as occasion serves and as need requires.

All similes of course fail us sooner or later, but they help us quite considerably on our way. Opposites do combine and may sound in and through each other, making differences which are more readily experienced than expressed. Our treatment of them cannot be complete, but it may be suggestive.

The Keynote of All.—The key to which all our ministry of reconciliation is set is unmistakably given to us in the great

Apostolic word in 2 Cor. 5. Our Gospel tones are to be sounded " In Christ's stead " and " As though God did beseech men by us." If we do not say, as Matthew Henry sometimes did, that " The key is on the door," we can, at any rate, say that " The key to which all the music is set is plainly marked on the staff at the beginning." Dr. Weymouth's rendering of Paul's passage in Rom. 10 is suggestive, too, of what is indispensable to the true conveyance of our Gospel message : " How shall they believe in One whose voice they have not heard ? " It is *His* voice which must sound itself in our delivery of His truth. The dead are to hear *His* voice : the sheep He must bring are to hear *His* voice. And in Longfellow's words, " That voice still soundeth on from the centuries that are gone to the centuries that shall be," sounding not least in the tones of our voices speaking " in His stead."

Sounds may be impersonal, but not so a voice. A voice gets its resonance from the whole person behind it. The " follow through " of that voice into the tones of our Gospel proclamation is surely involved, too, in our Lord's commission to His followers on the first Easter night : " As the Father hath sent me, even so send I you," as also in Luke's opening sentence in the Book of Acts : " The former treatise have I written of all that Jesus began to do and to teach."

It is a sobering question we should all ask ourselves : Is our generation really hearing *His* voice through our corporate fellowship and in our personal transmission of His Gospel ? And may it not be, that if men really heard His voice, through us, the dead would awake, and His other sheep be brought into the fold ?

The Tones of Graciousness and Authority.—The first impression our Lord's own ministry created was that of graciousness and authority. When He preached at Nazareth, where He was brought up, the wonder created was by the gracious words that proceeded out of His mouth. And the comment made about the Sermon on the Mount was that He spake as one having authority, and not as the Scribes.

Agape is the beating heart of the Gospel, and without it there is no Good News at all. Yet in that graciousness there is something which lays hold of us as by its own right. It is not the best thing we can think up, it is something given, and given in such a way that sovereignty sounds through it all. The existential element is at the heart of grace as well as of truth : " Love so amazing . . . demands . . ."

Graciousness and authority rest back on the tension in the heart of Holy Love—Love that must reconcile and rescue and yet must never surrender its rectitude, which can never deny itself.

The Psalms sound these notes, as indeed the whole Bible does. We get the Psalmist singing of mercy and judgment : of mercy and truth meeting together, and of righteousness and peace kissing each other. And in responsiveness he saw truth springing out of the earth, answering the righteousness which looked down from heaven. And it is by our communion with both the gracious and the austere aspects of these truths that we develop this blending in tone. Grace conceived too natural-istically without the element of judgment and authority in it, is toothless and has no bite. It is without its existential power of arrest. It has no strong pulse in it to precipitate decision.

On the other hand, authority may express itself in harsh notes unless tender grace suffuses it, and minds which always resist blank authority set up high walls of defence against it. We have no genuine Gospel tone if there is a lack of either the one or the other.

Our Lord's Emotions.—Deep communings with the heart and mind of our Lord are always needed if we are to speak in His stead and catch the tones of His voice. Our Lord's out-bursts of emotion ought to take us far into His inner life. His being moved with compassion is associated with His beholding of the multitudes and with His sight of heart-breaking sorrow. His jubilancy of spirit is over the gates of the Kingdom being opened to babes and sucklings whilst the secret of the Kingdom's life was hidden from the complacently wise and prudent.

His pent-up purposefulness showed in His face as His disciples followed Him on the way to the Cross—amazed.

His tension of spirit broke into visibility when the Greeks came seeking Him and He knew Himself to be at the crossroads of His ministry where the road He was called to tread led to the shadows of the Cross. His spirit was straitened as He thought with urgency and poignancy about His baptism of blood.

His anger blazed forth over those who would not enter the Kingdom and who kept others out. There were those deep sighs and groans, too, which escaped from Him at the sight of human handicaps and helplessness.

And there was much more if we can but read sympathetically between the lines. Robert Louis Stevenson used to say, " What you cannot vivify, omit." A variant of that counsel would be : What you sympathetically sense, include—even when there is not chapter and verse for it. George Macdonald believed as we do, that all God intended us to take from Holy Writ was not all in the letterpress—" If it had not been so I would have told you." And truly there is much one can catch here which breaks through language, and escapes. To mention only one thing in parenthesis as we pass on : Can anyone of us think that our Lord could ever " break the bread and bless it " without emotion ? Would it not call forth deep feeling of His body broken for our sakes, and would not the breaking of the bread bring its own peculiar and spiritual tension to His sinless, suffering heart ?

The Tones of Compassion and Compunction.—To beseech men in Christ's stead will involve our fellowship with Him in the deep places of His compassion and compunction. Men's helplessness drew Him to them, yet His pure spirit made Him weep and sigh over their sin and perversity. The attraction and repulsion must have created a mystic tension in His breast. His crown of thorns was lifelong. Our compassions are often without compunction because the sharp edges of our consciousness of sin have been blunted.

Our Lord's compassions were the costliest things because He bore the sicknesses He healed and was burdened under the sins He forgave. His eating with publicans and sinners was not in terms of the easy geniality of social intercourse. He bore the ache of His Father's heart as He consorted with them—the ache caused by the absence from His fellowship of His wandering children.

Paul entered very deeply into what he calls " the fellowship of Christ's suffering." Compassion burnt in him like a consuming flame as he cried :

" O to save these, to perish for their saving,
Die for their life, be offered for them all."

He experienced, too, a compunction, in some sense peculiarly his own, because of his past :

> " Dear men and women whom I sought and slew,
> O when I meet you in yon heavenly places
> How will I weep to Stephen and to you."

We all deplore how little of tender solicitude and yearning pity enters into our mediation of the Gospel. Von Hugel used to hold that " concern " was the distinctive Christian emotion. We often sing " Jesus, Thou art all compassion," but how little of that surging emotion we can lay claim to. How much do we really care—as the really great souls care? Dr. J. Alexander Findlay sometimes suggests that our Lord's strong crying and tears and His experience of dereliction was His spiritual and sympathetic identification with lost souls in their lostness. He was with lost souls as they took their lonely way in the dark.

A deeper fellowship with Christ in His sufferings would put a new and tender depth into our tones.

The Tones of Urgency and Poignancy.—We are surely meant to see ourselves represented in the king's servants bidden to go out quickly to bring in the halt and the blind—those who could not see their way, and those who were handicapped in taking it. And just as surely, poignancy is indicated in the heart of the king over the empty seats when such lavish provision had been made for so many. The notes here assuredly are, no time must be lost, all must be welcomed, for no cost had been spared. How often, in how many ways, one gets in the New Testament the impression that *what is total and final in God's gift must be fateful in any man's refusal of it.*

We must really deepen our sense of the tragic import in our Lord's words about " the outer darkness," and what our Lord meant by being " lost," and what is pictured in the New Testament about " perishing." When we have a fuller experience of " the life which is life indeed," we shall feel more deeply how " souls in the dark are undone "—going to pieces for want of the only constituent principle that can keep them together. " Lost," like wandering sheep and birds in pitiable plight, like displaced persons wandering homeless in the dark, perishing from want of cover and from lack of life's true bread ; and living in a nondescript world instead of the Father's world of love and light.

Time is a vital factor in all rescue. If it is not Now, it may
be Never. For souls have their seasons as have the fields and
the birds. And the harvest may pass and the migratory bird's
flight may be in the winter, when its wings are frostbitten.
These seasons come : we cannot buy them or bring them—and
we may miss them. One time is as good as another, is the
enemy's word. The Holy Spirit saith " To-day."

Poignancy may come into our souls and tones in more ways
than one.

> " That I should such a life destroy,
>   Yet live by Him I killed."

>   .   .   .

> " O why so late did I Thee know,
>   Thee, lovelier than the sons of men."

Dr. Forsyth's experience is classical. He never felt sin in its
horror and nauseousness, whilst he merely saw its workings
in his own spiritual history—for the more we are accustomed
to sin, the less we know it. He only saw sin with poignancy
when he saw it laid on the sinless and selfless Son of Man—
and then he was turned from a lover of Love into a lifelong
penitent, an object of grace and an evangelist.

Tones that both Haunt and Woo.—Or if again, we can
see ourselves as the children of the Bridechamber or as the
friend of the Bridegroom, surely we shall catch the tones of this
Tremendous Lover and sound out notes that both haunt and
woo. There is an ultimacy about this inexorable love which
will not let us alone.

And there is an allurement in its graciousness which draws
men, even despite themselves. And men's souls are drawn by
this Lover of our Souls and pursued by this Hound of Heaven.
They are not without some consciousness of this thrill and
thrall, but we are to exhibit both in our mediation on Christ's
behalf.

Paul felt them both. He was moved by the terror of the Lord
and by the constraining love of Christ. Both of these are aspects
of the one love : as George Macdonald puts it : " The terror
of the Lord is love storming the heart from without, using
every device to get inside." Love's constraint is that same love
revealing its irresistible urge from within.

Sometimes a legitimate criticism of our Gospel preaching is the criticism which Dr. Denney's wife passed on his—there was more power in it than pathos—" O, James (she would say), do take care how you use those hands."

What a difference it would make to our preaching if we realised that every man's heart, like Anathoth, is a home of the echoes and every man whose heart had closed against Christ had a love-haunted heart.

Renan, after he had left the Christian fold, confessed to soundings in his heart which were like the fabled buried Bells of Is of his native Brittany.

Elmore More, the American Platonist, having fallen to the fascination of Plato's Forms, felt at length that they began to pall, and in the hour of his loneliness he yielded to the haunting fascination of a Face.

And more recently, A. J. Cronin tells of his return to the Faith he had denied in answer to the echoes of a haunting voice within him, which would not be denied.

The Notes of Certitude and Jubilancy.—When the Apostolic note was sounded in the story of the Acts, we are told that men took knowledge of the sounders of it that they had been with Jesus. One wonders whether it was not the certitude and jubilancy with which they uttered their word that provoked the comment—and the compliment.

These two must go together. Certainty without jubilance is shrill and harsh. Jubilancy without certainty is corybantic. Certitude is the fruit of deep communing with truth, and jubilancy is the bloom on it. It is when they complement each other that they make an irresistible impression.

I once asked Dr. Maltby if he would let me use certain things he had said in something I was writing. With smiling face he said, " Yes, anything I ever said or wrote." The words I wanted were these : " God comes out of the inaccessible and presents Himself in such a way *that a man may know that he knows God* in Christ. I heard a man who had no such certitude. He gave me the impression of possessing a hesitant, divided, reluctant mind. He was like a Conservative Lord Mayor proposing the health of Ramsay Macdonald and trying to forget he was a Conservative, and to remember he was Lord Mayor."

In contrast to that absence both of certitude and jubilancy, many may remember Dr. Maltby's own account of a service he once held in Brunswick Chapel, Newcastle-upon-Tyne. In the prayer meeting a local magnate and Circuit Steward seated in the back pew so far forgot himself—to the shame of his family who gave him their black looks—as to walk all alone with enraptured face down the aisle towards the front as they sang to one of those tunes which circle round and round and never seem to end,

> " And all the attributes of God
> Are now at work for me. . . ."

For this kind of mediation we need first the *sense of grip*—the consciousness that our hand is closing on something real and objective, and then the sense that this Reality one holds and which is holding us is vibrant and resilient with its own Life and is communicating itself to us.

We then speak as though joy did make us speak—as those, too, who feel that we are not dealing with enemies to be laid low, but with friends we are to lift up.

The Closing Phase of the Study.—It might be well for us to consider together, in all too great incompleteness and brevity, in the closing phase of this study, some application of what has been already claimed. We ought to ask ourselves in all serious-ness this : What does this threefold character of the Redeeming Truth of the Gospel—dynamic, purposive, and personal—really mean for us in the three contexts in which it is set—the fully personal, the truly corporate, and the significantly global?

A useful clue to this consideration may perhaps be found in the closing phase of an ancient preacher's dolorous discourse on " The Illusion of Life." The truth we present is mercifully not of that sombre kind, but rather of the kind to relentlessly challenge that pessimistic view. Our message is of life with a capital L ; life in its fullest enrichments and enhancements.

Nevertheless, the point he makes—or the pious annotator makes for him as he draws to a close—is a very pertinent one. Truth, he seems to say, by its nature has a dual office, and calls for a dual expression in any who would communicate it. It is a goad and a nail. Its nature and office are to stimulate and challenge, and also to establish and to make steadfast and unify.

Both goads and nails are purposive instruments with pointed and piercing characteristics. They work by direct action and not by any round-about course. Both, too, become effective only when personal pressure is brought to bear upon them, by either immediate or mediate ways.

We do not doubt at all, as the Apostle says in another con-nection—and to change the simile for a moment—that the Spirit of God uses many instruments of mediation. There are many voices of the truth in this world, and none of them is without signification. Other things, he says, without life give sounds, as do the pipe and the harp. But he goes on to say, most evidently thinking of the truth of the Gospel—" If the trumpet give an uncertain sound, what then? " The voice the seer on Patmos heard was as the sound of a trumpet. And the purposeful, challenging, rallying note of the trumpet best befits our primal conception of Gospel truth.

Truth in its Dual Office.—Truth, in its impact on life, has often, if not always, this primal characteristic as a probe and as a stimulation. Socrates called himself the gad-fly of Athens, and the discourses of Pericles were said to have their sting in their tail.

In all conviction by the truth, it is this quality which is generally felt first. It is always so when we are in flight from Reality as Saul was on his way to Damascus.

It is significant, however, to notice that the goad which stopped his process of evasion when he kicked against it, when applied by himself to himself in later days, quickened his progress on towards the prize of his high calling.

It seems a sound principle to affirm that in the fine delicacy which should exist in all personal relationships, the point and probe of the truth—even in its punitive aspect—should be pressed upon our own heart first, and then only mediately and indirectly upon the hearts of others.

The only reprimands others are likely to heed are those we have already passed upon ourselves. I think there must be something of the suggestion of this in our Lord's words about not coming into the world to condemn the world. Besides, is not the very heart of the Gospel this—that God in the person of His Son made judgment sound its doom in His own heart first, and out of His bearing sin's judgment comes our own deep conviction of sin. I wonder if ever our fellows will come to a sense of the sinfulness of sin till they see us in some real way eating the sin-offering ourselves. The prophet Ezekiel, who was both a Watchman and an Omen, always seems to me to picture the true Mediator of the Truth, and if I were asked to set up a new picture of Interpreter in Interpreter's House, it would be of the kind represented by a sentry-man General Slim knew, who stood on his watch with his fixed bayonet *under his own chin* lest he should become slumberous at his post and endanger the lives of his fellows.

Where Truth Points Itself First.—This principle as to where Truth points itself first is supremely important. It is the only way to keep our sincerity and to save ourselves from censoriousness and professionalism.

Not only must the patient minister to himself, but as the Apostle suggests, the athlete must buffet his own body in this kind of conflict. It has been said that the mark of true genuineness in Christian living is to be ready to blame ourselves first. David never reaches a finer height in sainthood than when he lets Shimei continue casting dust and cursing him.

I always delight in two stories illustrative of this same principle. When John Wesley travelled on the stage coach with a passenger who annoyed everybody with his swearing, he took him aside when the inn was reached and said to him quite gently, " If you should find me using bad language on the next stage, I wish you would call my attention to it and reprove me." It is on the same line, too, that he affirmed that he never spoke to people about their sins without holding his own before his eyes. It is perhaps well known how Abraham Lincoln answered the murmurer who told him that a member of his Cabinet—Seward —had called him " A big fool." Stretching himself to his full height, he said, " You don't mean to tell me that Seward said that ? " " Yes," said the informer, " I heard him myself." " Then," said the President, " Seward may be right. I shall have to think about it."

The inner course Truth takes is always determinative of its outer circuit. If Truth is held up at its first step, it does not take a second.

Truth in its Constructive Ministry.—Like many others of my brethren, I am grateful that the New Testament in its delineations of Christian truth countenances all variations of metaphor in dealing with its many aspects. In one notable passage we, having received our Saviour as Lord, are to walk in Him and to be rooted in Him and built up in Him. Any schoolboy could criticise the clash of metaphor, but the saint knows how a deep appreciation of the Truth requires them all.

Truth becomes both constructive and creative as we bow to it and serve it. To get it to serve *us*, however, we must acknowledge its sovereignty and own its sway. It makes princes of us only as we let it conquer us. For in dealing with it, it is always dealing with us, and to it and to Him, every knee must bow. So truth at the same time as it offers its service, demands our submission and support. Because it stands in relationship with all life, we must relate it if it is to live.

Judge Waddy, I believe, used to say that truth was like a sock which would not stand up of itself: it needed a foot in it. It is not enough to affirm that truth will win the day. It will if we stand up in it, if we clothe ourselves in it. It will not stand up for itself. It is a potential on its way to become a power. It is a dynamic, but we may tie up its quickening energies. It is a personal relationship, but we must honour the principle of reciprocity as we must needs do in all such relationships.

A nail is inoperative in and of itself. Personal and persistent pressure must be applied to drive it home and give it the chance to be of stabilising service to us. And often, if not always, that contribution is made in the hidden places of the mind and heart. It pierces us to get in, and then supports us—strengthening, settling.

As Mrs Browning reminds us in one of her poems when she uses this metaphor: " The nail that holds the wood must buried lie."

Truth in its Personal Impact.—I guess we can all find ourselves in Maclardie Bunting's hymn (Methodist Hymn Book, 296) and in T. B. Pollock's (Methodist Hymn Book, 741). I remember the deep feeling Dr. Luke Wiseman showed when, in a company of ministers nearly thirty years ago, he asked us to sing the first-named hymn prayerfully and penitently. We all must give the truth its direct incidence in its personal impact on us. How often I, like the rest, have put on rubber gloves in dealing with this " live " thing. We have been willing to discuss and debate every aspect of the truth except in the particular relationship where it progged us. How Hellenic rather than Hebraic we have been in this matter : how often we have taken the edge off the instruments of God by our evasions and escapes. Our religious difficulty, like that of other people, has been the difficulty of being religious. Some of us make a liturgical escape, others a literary, others of us a lackadaisical. We are

ready with our J.E.P.D. while we and the world stand in
jeopardy every hour. We know the formula of the living water
and we put our H_2O to it, but we are thirsty still, and have not
got the pulse of the Fountain in it. We can reel off our H_2SO_4, but
the fire does not burn in our bones. We do not get the heat
through the formula. We all know—though I don't at the
moment—the formula for reviving air, and yet we are out of
breath, spiritually, which reminds me of what Dr. Maltby
said when Methodist Union was about to be consummated:
" In our Union together we shall have a bigger trumpet, but
shall we have the breath to blow it, or will it be that instead of
waking the dead we shall only disturb the neighbours ? "

God's Word to Jeremiah in that revelation by dialogue, is a
searching one, " If thou take the precious from the vile, thou
shalt be as my mouth." How often have I reminded myself of
Dr. Denney's words: " No man with a grievance can ever
preach the Gospel of Christ." We are to be the " Sons of
Kohath," carrying the ark of God's holy truth and presence
and promise on our shoulders. We can delegate the haberdashery
to the oxen and the wheels. The ultimacies of the Truth in all
their existential force must be brought both into our experience
and into our exegesis.

The Truth and Our Corporate Fellowship.—It has
always seemed meaningful to me that the parables, like Hebrew
poetry, seem to answer the movement of the feet and complement
each other. I have no opportunity to develop this, save to say
that the parables of the soils and that of the seeds go together.
There is a difference of the soils in one case and a difference of
the seeds in another—wheat and tares. And our Lord, in
commenting on the latter says: " The good seed are the children
of the Kingdom." When the Son of Man sowed the seed—it
was tested and selected seed. When the children of the Kingdom
are sown, they are a mixed bag. I remember in my boyhood
hearing J. B. Bayliffe—an honoured name to me and to many—
sound out the challenge from this parable: " Are we worth
perpetuating? Would the field of the world be better if filled
with our sort? Would the angels find any difficulty in recog-
nising us for what we are? " We all know the exceeding care
taken to get good seed. Thousands of pounds are spent every
year in their selection and test. May we not ask of our Corporate
Fellowship: " Are we really taking the necessary measures to

keep the Kingdom quality in the seed? In another sense than the prophet intended, can we imagine " He shall see his seed— and the travail of his soul in it—and be satisfied." I have little faith myself in *imposed* disciplines in our fellowship, though John Wesley imposed them and they have their place. In such exercises there is so great a danger of uprooting the wrong things. I have, however, tremendous faith in the self-imposed disciplines of our intensive fellowships, and there would be little need to impose regulations if we would only meet together in the healthful temper of relentless self-criticism and in the equally wholesome temper of boundless charity divine.

Old Jacob in dying said that Issachar would bow between two burdens. In our Corporate Life we must, too,—between the burdens we can share with one another, and the burden of our responsibility and concern which no one can share with us.

The Truth in its Widest Context.—An old missionary in China used to ask his audiences when he was on furlough what they thought was the most thickly populated valley in the world. Generally, of course, he got the answer " The Yangtse Valley," or " The Valley of the Thames." He would then say, slyly, " None of these. The most thickly populated valley is the Vale of Weeping." If I had been there in my present state of mind, I would have said " the Valley of Decision." For surely, as we look round in every part of the world, we see what Joel saw in his day, " Multitudes, multitudes in the valley of decision." And as in the words themselves, you seem to hear the hum and tramp of a countless host. The whole world to-day is a Valley of Jehosaphat, and the call is not only to take sides, but to bring such decision into our life and fellowship that men will feel the challenge ringing out from us. This is a time for greatness, and we are not as yet great enough for the hour. Dr. Denney used to say " The Gospel wins by its magnitudes," the something big that calls for the something big from others. We have not taken the call of this decision hour deeply enough upon our hearts ; and as a consequence we have not put on as yet the shoes of the preparation of the Gospel of peace. But we are going to do, by the mercy of God, and prepare ourselves by our intensive fellowship not only for communion with the Truth, but the communication of it.

I always delight myself in Rowland Hill's story, that he felt the urgency of the situation of human need so greatly that he ran out with only one shoe on. He went as a deacon, not being ordained as a priest, and anyway, with one shoe or without any, we must go into all the world in all its complex life and preach the Gospel to every creature.

The Last Word.—I remember a speaker who had only a minute left to speak, for the bell had just rung, saying, " I want to say this before I go : and I don't want to go before I say it." His feeling is mine. And what I say must both of necessity and by inclination, be in simile.

When our Lord said, " Now is the judgment of this world . . . and I, if I be lifted up, will draw all men unto Me," was not He saying that by bearing on His own heart the judgment of this world, He would provide what would be the irresistible attraction of the Cross ? And we only really lift Him up as we leave our own hearts open to that same judgment. It is that Cross, too, which must tone our fellowship.

They say that a great bell in China lost its tone, and the sages said that it must be re-cast, and that human blood must mingle with the metal. The tone rang true after that. Nothing will bring back tone into our Christian life and witness but *that something* which is the lifeblood of the Cross.

I once heard Dr. W. M. Macgregor tell of a saintly lady who in the Highlands had a cross erected on a height overlooking her estate, so that she and all who passed might see it. Years rolled by, and the undergrowth on that hilltop so surrounded the cross that you might pass by that way without ever noticing there was a cross at all. We must never let that happen in our personal or corporate life.

And finally, all our Evangelism must rest on and have its assonance in " the given." Rev. Roderick Bethune of Edinburgh told us the other night a true story of an episode in an Edinburgh hospital. A surgeon about to operate on an old man noticed a peculiarity about his hands, and asked what trade he followed. He was a cooper, and followed the Scottish fishermen. " Were you ever in Shetland, and did you once rescue a little boy and run away without giving your name ? " " I did," he replied. " Well, I was that little boy, and no one knew who had made the rescue except that they said he was a man with six fingers on one hand. So now I have found out my saviour. You did your best for me in my desperate need, and I am going to do my best for you now."

The Holy Spirit in Christian Experience and Evangelism

A POINT I think well worth making as an introduction to our study is that the doctrine of the Holy Spirit is not an annex or mere adjunct of our Christian faith, but the indispensable complement and crown of it.

This we may try to illustrate along certain lines. We must all have noticed how one gift of God needs another to complete it. The Christian year in its sequence seems always to bespeak this. No one gift is complete in itself. It is part of a series leading to a climax. And whilst on the one hand, God never goes back on His gifts, He always goes forward from them, as " the Ongoing God."

The old story of Caleb's wedding dowry to his daughter suggests the way the Heavenly Father deals with His children. The gift of the south land with all its prospects and possibilities would have been largely valueless without the further gift of the springs of water. And would not God's former gifts be vain without this further gift of His Spirit ?

Our Lord's call in His sermon for " *the more* " in the realm of loftier living and sonship character makes necessary His pledge to give " *the more* " in the enrichment and endowment of human nature by His Spirit.

Besides, it seems to be one of God's ways of making Himself indispensable to His children to make one gift of enrichment an embarrassment, and so He keeps us His petitioners whilst He is always equally bent on making us His partners.

43

George Macdonald's lines suggest the same truth :—

> God gave His child, upon a slate, a sum
>   To find eternity in hours and years.
> With both sides filled, back His child doth come,
>   With dim eyes swollen with unshed tears.
> God smiled, wiped clean the upper side and nether,
> And said, " Come, child, we'll do this sum together."

God's Gifts and their Gradations.—Then may we not also say that God's gifts have their gradations, all of which, in sequence, move to their climax.

The Word in ancient times was made in fragmentary parts and in prophetic glimpses. Then in the fulness of time the Word was made flesh and dwelt amongst us. In the person of His Son, God " pitched His tent " amongst us. In the ministry of our Lord, the Word became guidance—" The Life was the Light of men." In the Cross, the Word became vicarious. He who knew no sin became sin for us—identifying Himself not only with our life and lot, but with our sorrows and our sin, accepting sacrificially our plight in all the full range of its consequences, and offering Himself to God in our flesh and on our behalf, so putting away sin by the sacrifice of Himself.

In the Resurrection, the Word became victorious, spoiling principalities and powers by making a show of them openly. By His Ascension the Word became final. When He had purged our sins He sat down on the throne of the majesty of the Most High—God giving His imprimatur to His work and setting His seal on Christ's standard of righteousness.

Then in the Gift of the Spirit the Word became dynamic. In the experience of believing men, the Word becomes the engrafted Word, the reinforcing Word, the renewing Word, the searching Word, and in the realm of history and in the heart of unbelieving men, the Word becomes the Convicting Word, convincing men of sin and of righteousness and of judgment.

And in the Coming of the Spirit, what is historic becomes also super-historic. What is revealed is implemented ; what is potential is made realisable in all the wide ranges of the inner life of man.

We Need All the Contexts.—Another way of making the same point would be to say that our Christian faith only works as it is set in all its contexts. It takes all the checks to make the tartan, and it takes all its contexts to complete Christian truth.

It is common ground that Christianity rests on " *the given*." What is not so fully realised is that it rests on " all the given." John Ruskin used to say that he was not surprised at what men suffered, he was surprised at what men missed.

Was it not this that John Wesley missed before his Aldersgate Street experience. He had missed one of the contexts. In some sense he had been a spectator of the Divine nature without realising he was privileged to be a participator of it. General Gordon confessed that he missed this context in his earlier Christian life, too.

Wheeler Robinson in his book on the Holy Spirit did the same. In a certain illness of his he suffered from deep depression and felt that his Christian faith was yielding him less comfort and support than it ought to do, and he was led to see that he was missing this context of the Christian faith in the truth of the Spirit.

We need all the contexts—the Judean Hills, the Galilean Lake, the Green Hill far away, the empty Tomb. We need all that the written Word can give us as a basis for our faith. But we need, too, the Super-historic context which brings all the value and vitality of eternal life into personal experience. The Christ at the right hand of God must become the Christ of the heart, incorporating the eternal with the temporal in the innermost chambers of the spirit.

For in the Spirit, eternal life is not only at the end of the days but at the heart of them. The ageless life is not only the goal of our striving, but the spring and source of them. Christ's renewing and satisfying life, through the Spirit, becomes " a fountain springing up " with an impulse beating with the pulse of its Eternal Source.

The Contexts Fertilise Each Other.—Again, since these contexts are all in the living whole in which the Spirit operates, they fertilise one another. These contexts mate. There is not only interplay between them, they pollinate each other. The historic helps to bring to flower the inward realisation of the truth through the Spirit's operation in both. The inner experience fertilises the sacred records through the same spirit.

D

Historic facts become impregnated with eternal quality and become faculty ; text becomes texture.

Fiehte is reported to have said that we are saved by the metaphysical—the idea—rather than by the historic. Rather we are saved by the fertilising of the truth which is both experience and history.

And the true glory of our Christian faith is that we do not laboriously fetch and carry from the well that is historic (though the historic may be as highly regarded as was Jacob's well at Sychar), the water Our Lord gives is the water of a springing fountain, which not only quenches the thirst of one, but has its overflow into the life of the many. And reading this saying in the 4th chapter of John, I am tempted to say as Dr. Maltby once said in another connection, " It was only by an inadvertence that the fourth evangelist did not put in his parenthesis here, as he did in the 7th chapter." This spake He of the Spirit which they who believe on Him should receive ; for the Holy Spirit was not yet given, because that Jesus was not yet glorified.

Some day, perhaps, there may arise someone who may do for us what Linnaeus did for horticulturists in his *Floral Nuptials* and work out on a spiritual level the Spirit's operation in the pollination of the Christian graces by bringing together in mystic mating one living context with another.

The Gift of the Spirit : Our Lord's Trophy.—It is perhaps only another way of making the same claim, to say that the Holy Spirit is at once the gift Christ won by His victory and the pledge of every future triumph of His Church.

This suggestion always seems to be conveyed by the picture of Isaiah 40 in which Israel's Deliverer coming with a strong band shall bring the spoils of victory with Him. " His reward is with Him and His work before Him." Peter on the day of Pentecost in his sermon links together Christ's victory with " the shedding forth of this." The victory won has this gift as its greatest trophy. And all the endless track before is to be undertaken in the reinforcement of what is both trophy and pledge. It is " from victory unto victory " we are to march as our Lord leads us. The Church must always be a langorous body, moving with uncertain and hesitating tread if it marches only " unto " victory. It must march " from " it to be all victorious. The fruits of victory must already be experienced before we step out, or our step will be that of the weary and the easily tired. The light of victory must be in our eyes and the assurance of it in our hearts.

And indeed, it is but the truth to say that while our Lord inaugurated the New Charter of His Church in His Cross and Resurrection, that New Charter is only implemented by His Spirit. God puts His law within our minds and inscribes it upon the tablets of our hearts by the Spirit He has given unto us. By His Spirit He causes us to walk in His ways ; and when we see the early Church " walking in the Comfort of the Holy Spirit " and being edified and multiplying its converts, we get the picture of " the fully endowed " Christian Community.

The Terminology of the Doctrine.—The terminology of the doctrine of the Holy Spirit often befogs us. Whilst the Spirit is spoken of in personal pronouns, His operations are often referred to impersonally.

Then, while many unmistakably live in the Spirit and walk in the Spirit, they have not clarified their minds as to His person. " We do not acknowledge always in the top of our minds, much that we truly experience at the bottom of our hearts." Different names are given to the same thing. The same sea which in the east is the German Ocean, is on its western side the North Sea. The common salt at the table is sodium chloride in the laboratory. There seems little likelihood of any one of us distinguishing, in the realm of experience, the presence of the Living Lord from the Power of the Holy Spirit, since indeed " He shall not speak of Himself." Baptism with the Holy Spirit we associate with the historic act of Pentecost : the filling of the Holy Spirit with the experimental side of that outpouring. Coleridge has it, that most truths are aphorisms and that great men are aphorisms too. For us, Stephen with his uplifted and shining face and Barnabas with his magnanimous and generous temper, are " aphorisms " of the Spirit-filled life.

The enduement of the Spirit is His power operating in the Christian's life and ministry.

The sealing of the Spirit is God's confirmatory operation as by His imprimatur He evidences ownership of us, authenticates our sonship, and gives us protective security.

Whilst the " earnest of the Spirit is prophetic of that fuller fruitage which will be ours in Christian grace in the day of our perfected redemption."

The graces of the Christian life are fruits of the Spirit. Dr. Denney used to say that the Grecian graces were beauties, but all the Christian graces were both beauties and powers.

The Holy Spirit's Title.—The fact that the Holy Spirit bears the title of Spirit is of itself an indication of an affinity between the Spirit of God and the spirit of man—of a deep calling to the deep. The tragic fact that there is something other than affinity—alienation indeed—must not obscure from us the fact that the affinity is original and basic. There is the inner light and the inner darkness, but here, as elsewhere, " the darkness extinguisheth it not." Paul's argument in 1 Corinthians, 2nd chapter, seems based on the acknowledgment of this affinity, " What man knoweth the things of a man save the spirit of a man which is in him, even so, the things of God knoweth no man but the Spirit of God."

This affinity of Spirit with spirit, as Tennyson suggests in his *Higher Pantheism* has large consequences :

" Speak to Him, for He hears,
    And Spirit with spirit may meet ;
Closer is He than breathing,
    Nearer than hands and feet."

That eccentric genius, Laurence Oliphant, used to propagate the fancy that every man had his counterpart in the invisible order, and that a man's great business in living was to get into touch with his alter-ego and so crown and complete himself. The idea is not all fiction, for man's true counterpart is in the Spirit of God, and a man when filled with the Spirit is fully himself. As the Holy Spirit was in some real way Our Lord's Other-self, so He is also the necessary complement of every man's personality. For the truth about personality, as it has been truly said, is that we are not what we are in our bare selves, but all we can take hold of in the life of God and all that can take hold of us from the side of God. There must always be " a bare look " about any man who has not put forward his claim to his share in the life of God. And the only escape from the corruption of the world would seem to be, as we are " partakers of the divine nature."

The Spirit as Comforter.—The Spirit was to be Another Comforter ; to be, indeed, to the disciples all that Jesus had

Himself been to them in the flesh, in the way of reinforcement and good cheer.

Our Lord was always coming to His followers in their loneliness and dread, ministering support and bidding them to " Be of good cheer." And the Spirit was to stand by them as He had done. They would not be left as orphans without *invisible* means of support, but would be helped in every time of need. The Other Comforter would proceed with Our Lord's ministry where, to men's feeble sense, He seemed to have left off, and carry it forward to fullest realisation, inspiring them, teaching, guiding and empowering them in all their work and witness.

And He was the Comforter in the original sense of the word as One standing by in supporting strength, rather than as merely ministering consolation. Tyndale, I suppose, in his translation of a passage in Jeremiah speaks of a maker of idols " comforting it with nails."

This reinforcement and encouragement the Spirit brings to us by mediating to us in the range of personal experience that Eternal Life which our Lord brought to time and history in His own Personal Ministry of Life, Death and Resurrection.

The Epistle to the Hebrews makes reference to our Lord as having His credentials to His Priesthood not by Aaronic descent but by His possession of " the powers of an endless life."

And as it was through " the Eternal Spirit " that He offered Himself without spot to God, so it is through the same Eternal Spirit that He mediates the powers of the endless life to us, so making the ageless life interweave itself with time in the life of man. Man by the make-up of his nature is a texture formed by the warp and woof of the temporal and eternal, and the strength of the personal fabric is dependent on the Comforter's mediation.

The Spirit of Truth.—The Spirit of Truth takes the things of Christ and shows them unto us. Whatever other office in the wide ranges of truth the Spirit has, it is clear that His chief office is to unfold " the truth as it is in Jesus."

As bringing all things to our Remembrance and as showing things to come in special reference to that Truth, He makes the truth *contemporaneous*. As the Eternal Spirit operating from a realm which transcends the temporal, He links past and present and future. And so the Holy Spirit—as the Epistle to Hebrews puts it—always says " To-day." It is surely this which makes Truth live and relevant. Simon Peter on the day of Pentecost linked the past with the present when, at the inauguration of the Spirit's larger ministry, he said, " This is that." The past leapt in the Person of the Spirit upon the present. The Spirit is God's pontifex bridging all time.

The Spirit, too, makes this Truth *existential*. Through Him, it has power to arrest and convict. Because it belongs to the ultimate, it has ultimacy and delivers what is nothing less than its ultimatum in the human spirit. It demands from us not an easy acquiescence but an attitude and action.

We all know the kind of truth which is viewed with a mere nod of assent, about which we do nothing.

Dr. Johnson, in *The Rambler* of 1751, described a brooding philosopher who, on being told that fire was spreading destruction all around, composedly remarked that it was the nature of fire to operate in circles, and resumed his speculations.

Archimedes, too, it is said, was only awakened out of his speculative stupor when war raged in Syracuse by a soldier with drawn sword stepping on to one of his diagrams which rested on his study floor.

So the Spirit of Truth re-directs our minds from the mere past and from the purely abstract to the abiding and vital element in Truth. And Dr. Denney reminds us that the disciples never remembered Jesus, they experienced Him.

The Spirit of Truth makes Truth Progressive.—The Spirit, too, makes Truth *progressive*. The many things our Lord *would* have said to His disciples He entrusted to the Spirit. The norm of Truth is fixed, but there is a ceaseless unfoldment of it. In a deep sense the Spirit introduced our Lord to His ministry when " He returned in the Power of the Spirit into Galilee," and in a real sense, too, He continues that ministry in opening up the way for our Lord " To Him the Porter openeth."

No revision of the Truth as it is in Jesus is ever needed or possible, but the realisation if it is always needed and the relevancy of it to each succeeding situation requires to be seen.

Truth is always breaking forth from God's Holy Word, and from God's Holy Son and the Spirit undertakes this mediation.

Our peril is to " date " Christian Truth and to fight new battles with the weapons of the last.

There is also the constant peril of doing what the old man in Sante Beuve is said to have done, " stopped his watch at a given time," refusing to recognise any further advance.

Underlying all the words of our Lord about the Spirit of Truth is the implication that we are all the ready subjects of illusion. Illusions dictated by our prejudices and prepossessions and particularly our perversity and our pride. And this vicious circle of our self-enclosed world needs constantly to be assailed.

Carlyle once said about a certain man that he was engaged in plastering together the true and the false, and out of fashioning the plausible.

Our problem is always that of getting Truth to do its work in ourselves and in others. Sir James Stephen once asked why it was that truth which none could disprove fell so ineffectually on the ear and so seldom reached the heart. He held that it was because of the formidable alliance of sense and imagination. Who can break through such a vicious circle, such an unhallowed alliance but the Spirit of Truth who makes Truth contemporaneous, existential and progressive.

The Spirit's Operations.—We may view the Spirit's operations in a threefold way as implementing our High Calling, our Holy Calling, our Heavenly Calling in (1) Sonship ; (2) Sainthood ; and (3) Service.

In Sonship He creates the filial consciousness within us. He is the Spirit of freedom and fearlessness which rightly belongs to sonship. God sends forth His Spirit into our hearts, dispelling fear and foreboding and whispering " Abba." He so implements the Divine intention of " bringing many sons unto glory " and cancelling out in us the returning prodigal's feeling that a lower status as hired servants is more befitting such beggary as ours.

We do not think up this high call, we do not call ourselves sons as did the Wapping butcher, Arthur Ortor, in the famous Tichborne Case, to have it proved against us that we have neither the accent nor the background worthy of such a title. For the Spirit not only inspires in us the joyous consciousness of sonship giving us the ring and the robe and the feast, but He proceeds to form the sonship likeness in us by His continual presence in our hearts. " He owns me for His child, I can no longer fear "—sings Charles Wesley. He then proceeds to " scatter His life through every part to sanctify the whole " :

the name of sons is honoured by newness of life in both behaviour and bearing. We become " conformed to Christ's image. We are made new creatures in Christ Jesus." " The law of the Spirit of life in Christ Jesus makes us free from the law of sin and death."

And since a thing is not only what it is in itself, but all it leads to, our sonship involves inheritance so that " all things are ours." The son has the full freedom of the house. No cordoned off areas limit his freedom. There may be bounds set to servants, but not to sons who dwell in the Father's house. And it is the Spirit who opens out to us all the treasures of the Father's heart.

The Spirit's Operation in Sainthood.—The Spirit's operations in Sainthood are as manifold as is the grace and wisdom of God. " Come as the light, the fire, the dew, the dove, the wind—pleads the hymn—in all Thy gracious powers, O come, Great Spirit, come."

In *Searching*, the Spirit's activity is twofold. " The Spirit searcheth all things, yea the deep things of God." He gives us to know the " things which are freely given us of God." He opens out to us the depths of the wisdom and grace of God.

> " God, through Himself we then shall know
>   If Thou within us shine."

The Spirit searches, too, the thoughts and intents of the heart. He searches out our insincerities. The Old Testament tells of the searching of the Law, of searching Jerusalem with candles ; the searching of the Spirit in the New Testament is the tender, jealous searching of a love which brooks no rival. This seems to be the suggestion of the passage in the Epistle of James which says, " The Spirit that dwelleth within us loves with a jealous love." The Spirit as the executor of the Living Will of Christ and of the selfless love which took Him to the Cross will never grant us peace until our love in its intention and passion is undivided and entire.

What the Spirit says to the Seven Churches is indicative of this jealous searching love. He is sensitive to the lowered temperature of the affection of the Ephesian Church. He is intensely provoked by the self-complacent and self-congratulatory temper of the Laodiceans. He knows the unfulfilled works of the Church at Sardis which had crossed the dead line and had only a name to live. But always the searchings are the searchings of a Spirit whose love would not let go, and would not let down and would not let off : and never the searchings undertaken on the search-warrant of Law.

The Spirit in Support.—The Spirit continually supports and sustains us in all the practice and under all the pressures of sainthood. He is the Great Helper vocalising in our hearts the good cheer of Jesus Christ.

The operations of the Spirit in support are generally rendered in the deeper places of our subconscious life. How often we have discovered that " He giveth His beloved in sleep."

Dr. Johnson used to go on dark nights along the Thames Embankment and put coins in the hands of the ragged laddies sleeping there who, on awaking, were left in bewilderment and wonder how their needed help had come.

Robertson of Irvine had a famous sermon he would not have reported on " Moses wist not that his face shone "—in which he enunciated the principle that our own consciousness is an inadequate register of (1) What is coming to us ; (2) What is going from us ; and (3) and of What life is doing to us in the way of marring or beautifying our features. And to think of the first part only just now, how silently and secretly does God come to us through His Spirit, by way of the assimilative and associative mind. As the processes of digestion are secret, and as the way things seemingly forgotten are tossed back into our remembrance, so the Spirit works.

Mrs Meynell's children used to plead with their mother to come up to their room where they slept and leave some token of her coming behind, like a flower or a grape. So all unknown to us at the time, God leaves His fragrances and His tokens in our lives.

The poem of Longfellow set to music by Sir Edward Elgar tells of this ministry best :

" As torrents in summer, half dried in their courses,
    Suddenly rise though the sky above them is cloudless ;
For far off at their fountains the rain has been falling,
    So hearts that are weary grow full to o'erflowing.
And they who behold it marvel and know not
    That God at their fountains, far off, has been raining."

The Spirit in Guidance and Prayer.—The Spirit directs and guides both in personal life and in His Church. He initiates projects in men's hearts and minds by giving to them pulses not their own, that have the pulses as rivers have of the heights from which they rise. He operates both in the opening and closing of doors, as He did in the personal lives of Philip and Peter and Paul; and also in the community life of the believers when they separated men to their ministries under higher direction. Concerns we feel are of His inception, " stops in the mind " are part of His leading.

Supremely, too, He is the underswell of His people's prayers. He upbears both our worship and our intercessions on His breath as our breath upbears our speech and song.

He stands to support us in our infirmities in prayer, since we know not either how to pray or what to pray for.

Prayer we may say is a path, a school, and a ladder. " The path of prayer Thyself best trod, Lord teach us how to pray." " Prayer climbs the ladder," Jacob saw. And as we tread the path of prayer with uncertain feet, either privately or in company, His hand supports us. As we put an " L " in our window when we pray, He schools us in the exercise. As we take the ladder rung by rung from the lowly earth to the vaulted skies He steadies us as we climb.

When we fail to persevere He prompts us to go on. The great ground swell of the Eternal heart sounds its unutterable note as we open ourselves to His operations. The unspeakable yearnings of God Himself for men's lost souls tone themselves in our spirits as we, under His tuition and support, learn to pray.

And it is by " praying in the Holy Spirit " that we keep ourselves in the love of God and under His inspiring breath. We exult in it, expose ourselves to it, explore it, and express it, comprehending with all the saints " it's far-flung dimensions."

The Fruits of the Spirit.—The Spirit operates outstandingly in the creation of the Christian graces. These are none other than the virtues of Christ formed in us. All these fruits are distinctive, have a kindgom quality and, as bearing in them the powers of the endless life, are qualitatively different than their opposite numbers of the natural order.

The Grecian graces are here, and the Hebrew graces, but all distinctively Christianised. It is Agape, " Love divine all loves excelling " which marks the difference. This Love is not only a virtue, but the parent of them all. It begets its quality unfailingly in all the others.

Joy is the joy of the believing heart and has a buoyancy all its own, not being dependent on surrounding conditions, but being the true overflow of the fountain life of the ages.

Peace is not " as the world giveth," not to be identified with the inert and self-complacent temper. It is a peace as far removed as heaven from earth from " Nirvana," and is the Ataraxia of which our Lord spoke in the Upper Room.

The monks of the Middle Ages suffered from a strange malady which was called Accidia. It was a nausea of the soul which made all living tasteless, and all service tedious. It was surely the absence in their lives of this good Spirit of God who makes all things new and preserves the soul from tempers which pall.

The feminine and tender graces predominate among the nine, and more than Dr. Thomas Chalmers have been led to say that Longsuffering and Gentleness were amongst the most precious of the Spirit's fruits. The Love that endures all things, smilingly and patiently, is not a natural product, but is —with the others—a not-to-be-imitated Grace of the selfless and patient Spirit of God.

The Spirit in Service and Witness.—The self-same Spirit who makes Truth existential in the believing heart, gives an existential quality to our service and witness. He changes the indicative into the imperative. The Spirit's enduement makes all the difference between our mere arguing a case and our advocating a cause and mediating a conviction. F. W. H. Myers, born in the Keswick Vicarage, hearing Dr. Frederick Temple preach, sang :

> " For as he spake I knew that God was near,
>   Perfecting still the immemorial plan ;
> As once in Jewry and for ever here
>   Lives as He lives, ends where He began."

He was conscious of the mystic plus.

In the old days of the Thomas Willshaw Theological Class I remember Thomas Champness representing the Paraclete standing by us in this wise. The scene, he said, was a hostile

Court where a witness is embarrassed and hard bestead to make good his witness. He espies One in Court whom he knows and who will help him, and beckons to Him. This Other One makes His way unobtrusively through the crowded Court till He stands by his side. He whispers His confirmations to his embarrassed mind and corroborates his testimony, backing it with irresistible might so that the case which was going against the witness swings round and is turned to his favour.

The Operations of the Spirit are both distinctive and diversified. He distributes to every one severally as He will.

Some forty years ago I heard Dr. Horton preach on the Spirit clothing Himself in Gideon to give witness and win victory, and the same Spirit clothing Himself in Zecharias to make a protest and to suffer martyrdom. And, later, I was led to see how different it is " to cover a thing than to clothe it."

When a thing is covered the distinctive outline and features of it are lost. When anything is clothed the distinctive features are not only evidenced but enhanced. So the Spirit clothes us as His witnesses—sometimes to suffer, sometimes to labour—but always to mediate a life and passion other than our own on a personality that is truly our own.

The Conditions of the Spirit's Operations.—As to the conditions under which the Spirit operates in personal life and ministry, I would put *Openness* first. I mean the openness which is the opposite to self content and self concern : the openness of the displaced person who seeks to say with Paul, " I live yet not I." That openness is both susceptibility and receptivity, which two always go together, for we receive as we are susceptible and are susceptible as we receive.

Our Lord said, " Receive ye the Holy Spirit—open the heart to Him in welcome."

I suppose that in the early days of Empire building our British government would only ask of subject peoples not any tribute but only that they would keep their ports open to the traffic of the homeland.

If we leave room for the Spirit of God, He will not fail to fill the space we leave for Him. As the ocean rolls towards the shore flows into every creek and cranny, as the air fills any vacuum made available to it, so the Spirit will fill the nature which opens to Him.

With infinite delicacy and courtesy God leaves room for us, giving us living space, not crowding us out, but leaving us space to make our venture in living and our contribution in service. So with the same delicacy and courtesy we are called upon to leave room for God—as also for one another—not cramping His activity or limiting the Holy One of Israel.

J. P. Struthers used to delight to repeat, " Leave but a green bough for His feet and God will send His blackbird there."

Scores of times within recent years I have repeated over to myself and to others the lines of T. E. Brown, written as he picked up a shell on the Ramsey beach :

" If thou couldst empty all thyself of self
    Like to this shell dishabited,
  Then He might find thee on the ocean shelf
      And say, " This is not dead," and fill thee with Himself
      instead.

" But thou art so replete with very ' Thou,'
    And hast such shrewd activity,
  That when He comes, He saith,
    ' This is enough unto itself,
  'Twere better let it be.
    It is so small and full
  There is no room for Me.' "

To Them that Obey Him.—*Obedience* is the true correlative of openness and an indispensable condition of the Spirit's operations. " For openness is an invitation to God to enter and conform our minds to His loving, living will." And God, being an Ongoing God who is always calling us to keep in touch with His living will, we must subdue our spirit to obedience in discovering the way He is going ; and go that way. God's manifestations of Himself can never be fully expressed in the statutes of law, His mediations and His purpose are contemporaneous, and so we are called to conform. Mrs Pearsall Smith once said that the grandest Christian she ever knew said that the single rule of his life was " to let his obedience keep pace with his light."

This Obedience involves both *Abandonment and Abiding*. We let go our own hands from our gifts and powers to let His hands rest on them. And as in the story of the Feeding of the

Multitudes, the creative powers began to operate when things were brought. The lad took his own hands off his little store and the Lord's hands rested on what he brought. And as I once heard it said, there is a real significance in the sequence. " He took, He blessed, He broke, He gave."

We so often get in the way by failing to let ourselves go.

Dr. Denney's reminder is never out of place, " No man can witness to himself and to Christ at the same time. No man can give the impression that he is clever and that Christ is wonderful at one and the same time."

It *means Abiding, too*—making God our habitat and giving the Spirit of God His chance to incorporate eternity within our hearts. This must be what Paul meant by " dwelling in heavenly places in Christ." Hudson Taylor, it is said, as he left the Keswick platform, said impressively to Bishop Taylor Smith, " The secret of Christian living is in abiding."

In Experience and Evangelism " Committal."—It is perhaps only saying the same thing in different words to say that the condition on which the Spirit of God works both in experience and evangelism is *Committal*. It is the partially committed life which limits the Holy One of Israel. In the introduction to a Missionary Report I remember reading words which have deeply impressed me : " It is the way of the Spirit of God to break in upon human life and upon the human situation conspicuously, at the point of our committal." It is when we take a decisive step that the Spirit can release His power upon us and through us. The point of committal is the point of ignition. The fire falls when we go all out in our abandonment to God as it fell on Carmel.

Moses at the Red Sea had to countermand his order to " Stand still." The word for that crisis was committal. " Speak to the children of Israel that they go forward." That, of course, is not to say that the Spirit's breath is not in the inception of our plans, in young men's visions and in old men's dreams. He never fails in His initiatives. But these are but overtures which call for something from us. They are incomplete in themselves. The wonder of wonders is that though God might do without us, he does not choose to do. He would bring us into His forward movement, get us to go step by step with Him in His march.

And, as often is the case, it is in the absence of integration where lies the lag. The complex will be broken when we take a step forward.

Dr. Chalmers in a letter to his sister tells of the careworn look the 400 ministers had whilst they debated what their action should be in 1843. So long as they merely considered, they were burdened men. But when they took the critical step in committal these same men had a radiant look on their countenances.

The Spirit of God broke in conspicuously at the point of committal.

The Demonstration of the Spirit.—A quite important final consideration is the line and level on which we are to expect " the demonstration of the Spirit and of power " in our Christian witness. One thing is certain, it must be " in character " with the grace and truth which our Lord brought in all the range of His personal life and ministry. And seeing that grace and truth are manifold and newness of life is ever unpredictable, we are to look for its evidences in the creative rather than in the repetitive and reiterative. We are to look for it in the qualitatively different rather than in the externally similar.

On *our side*, it will be experienced in *kindling*, in the warmed heart, in the mating of the truth with life in its inmost texture. The Spirit of Truth will evidence His presence in our experience of realisation. And that sense of full assurance will often consort with much weakness and tremor as with the Apostle and not with self assurance and blatancy.

A yearning concern and a sense of irresistible constraint will characterise our experience, together with the sense Dinah Morris felt so deeply of " not being left to ourselves—of being attended."

On *the side of others*, there will be the sense of the irresistible impact of truth as something " live," of something lived in before being spoken about. Truth, if really communed with, will give unmistakable evidence of itself in its searching convicting power such as that which attended the witness of Stephen when the Sanhedrin could not resist the power and wisdom with which he spake.

Some may find the truth like the gentle dew and the sunshine and, like Lydia, open their heart to it. Others may resist the truth to their own hurt, and wreak their wrath on its witnesses. But always with the Spirit's accompaniment of the Truth there will be something effectual wrought and issues precipitated in the hearer's heart and mind.

We would be wise, however, to remind ourselves that the Spirit's power is persuasive and not coercive, and that the demonstration of the Spirit is in the normal and ordinary rather than in the outré.

Our Ministry of Mediation

In our personal life and in our corporate Christian witness the cardinal principle is surely mediation. Our Lord mediates His life to us by His Spirit, and we mediate His life to others in the ranges of our daily contacts and our corporate witness. The principle is from Life, through Life to Life. " The highest cannot be spoken," we are often told; it can, however, be mediated. Our life and witness is not merely " in His name " and on His behalf, but by the pulsings of our Lord's very life within our own.

Phillips' translation of the great words in the first Epistle of John—" As He is, so are we in this world "—are in strong support of this master principle. " The life we live in this world is actually His life in us." That means, as read on the context, not only that we shall be bold in the day of judgment as sharers in His life; it means that we shall be reproducing in very similitude that Life amongst men. The mediation will involve tension and adaptation, interpretation and indentification, because it is " in this world," but the veritable life of our Lord is to be expressed in us and through us.

We do well to remind ourselves that *Imitation* is not the central thing. That would be too mechanical. We are indeed " to imitate God as dear children." That is, as sharing the Divine Life. And as Dr. Stalker reminds us, a child is like his mother, not chiefly that he copies her ways and her gait, but because he shares his mother's life.

The cardinal principle is not *Impersonation* either. That would be too theatrical. The seven sons of Sceva tried it to their dismay and discomfort.

Nor is it that of *Representation*, though that is a much fuller and richer description of the relationship which we bear. Our representative capacity in the Christian life rests on the basis of the immediacy with which we share our Lord's risen life.

We are His representative men, not as deputising for Him, but as being joined to Him in one spirit, sharing and then communicating His life to others.

"Freely Ye have Received, Freely Give."—This principle is everywhere honoured in the New Testament.

We all know how frequently Dr. Maltby stressed the truth of the real conveyance of the peace and comfort of Christ through Christian lives. It is thirty years ago since I heard him in the St. Andrew's Halls in Glasgow at the Students' Missionary Conference depict how real this bestowal was. On the first Easter Sunday evening when He greeted His disciples He said what everybody said. It was the familiar greeting one wayfarer passes to another, " Peace be to you," but when He said it the Peace was there. When, too, at an earlier period he had sent out seventy of his friends on their first adventure in preaching, He gave them the instruction—" When you go into a house first say ' Peace be to this house,' and if there is a lover of peace there, your peace shall rest on them, and if not (so real a thing it is) your peace will come to you again. Like Noah's dove, it must rest somewhere." There is no mistaking this. No purse, no wallet, no spare sandals, but they are to carry peace and give it away. Paul, writing to the Philippians, says " I long for you all with a love that is not mine, but is Christ loving in me."

Comfort too, like peace and love, are communicable things to be mediated by us.

I have a vivid memory as a boy in my early teens hearing Frank Crossley of Ancoats during the Armenian atrocities as he leaned over the rails of the rostrum reading with deep feeling the great words in 2nd Corinthians—" Blessed be the Father of Mercies and the God of all comfort who comforteth us in all our tribulation, that we may be able to comfort them which are in any trouble by the comfort whereby we ourselves are comforted of God." The sufferings of Christ overflow into our lives it is true, but there is overflowing comfort, too, which Christ mediates to us.

It always seems significant to me, too, that in John's record of the first Easter evening, it was immediately after our Lord had breathed His Spirit and His peace upon His disciples, He followed it by saying—" As the Father hath sent Me, even so send I you " to be bearers of His spirit and His peace.

We Deal with Communicable Things.—We are as Christ's men to be " like celestial bagmen, uncommercial travellers, with a store of spiritual gifts delivering the goods." We deal with communicable things. We do not merely talk about love and joy and peace. We carry them and offer them. It is our vocation to mediate them. We are Christophers. It is of His fulness we have all received and grace for grace—grace in us answering to grace in Him—that we might mediate it.

Peter's great passage delineating the high privileges and holy prerogatives of the new Israel God's people sets all that [almost unbelievable distinction and dignity in the context of the Church's mediation of God's excellences to the world, " Ye are, that ye may." The high calling of God in Christ Jesus is not in any sense whatsoever, to be viewed as a perquisite to be treasured for ourself, but as an enrichment to be made available for all. And it is the whole Church in the priesthood of all believers and as the new race that is the mediating body.

This is all part of what Paul calls " the ministration of the Spirit." And in that ministration we are channels not cisterns, conveyers not containers. We are to join together in the service of our lives the fulness we have received with the emptiness and poverty of the world around us.

As the Panama Canal channels the pulses of the Atlantic into the Pacific, and that of the Pacific into the Atlantic ; as the Suez Canal bears the waters of the Mediterranean to the Red Sea and Indian Ocean, so our ministration and mediation are to link together what would else be separated and apart.

It is the way of Grace to abound, to overflow ; and the overflow is to be in and through us.

There used to be a little man at the Southport Convention who was accustomed to pray—" O Lord, Thou knowest we cannot hold much, but we can overflow a lot."

Personality, our Inflow and Outflow.—It is quite in keeping with this principle of mediation that our personalities are constituted that way. There is a continuous inflow and outflow which characterises them. We are not self-contained, like marbles in a box ; rather we are like a stream with inflowing contributory influences and outgoing effluences. Without realising it often, this dual action is continually operating in our lives. And what is more, it is the inner quality of our being which is being released and mediated day by day.

We never really do anything else in living than " give ourselves away." It is not the extraneous things which find expression, but our essential self.

Hudson Taylor had a most original way of communicating this principle to his newly appointed Missionaries. He would meet his men at a Chinese port and take them into some nearby restaurant for a meal and for conversation. He would direct the conversation to the conditions under which they would require to carry on their work, the hostility they would most certainly encounter, and then, without warning, he would strike the table sharply, spilling some of the beverage they were drinking. Then shrewdly and smilingly he would say: " But remember, you will only spill over with what is really inside you." If tender compassion is in your heart, you will spill over in forbearance and forgiveness and not with resentment.

Our Lord, when reviled, reviled not again. His heart could only love, and we must be like Him, sharing His life and temper in our service.

And in the quality of our life and service, God in Christ is to be made palpitatingly real and accessible and lovable to men.

We are to spill over with this quality of life. In us, as in Christ, God must never be far away. In us, as in Christ, God must be exhibited as never disdainful but always compassionate. In us, as in Christ, God must be expressed as full of grace and truth.

The Mediation of Grace and Truth in Wonder.—As a great master spirit—a composer or organist—makes use of every manual of his organ, and even the pedals, to interpret his theme and mediate his message, so personally are we to manifest and mediate the grace and truth of Christ to men in the full range of our gifts and powers.

We are to mediate it first in the *Wonder* with which we envisage it. The sense of the marvellousness and miracle of the Gospel must never become dimmed in our imagination. It is nothing less than a tragedy when we view our salvation prosaically. Indeed, we cease to preach the Gospel when we recover from the wonder of it.

How constant was this sense of amazement breaking through the Apostles' speech—" To me . . . less than the least is this grace given." Part of the facility, too, with which the the truth, we preach, is borne to our hearers, is in the wonder it has awakened within our own minds and hearts. The mystery and marvel of the truth is such that nothing is true about it which is not coloured—it is manifold grace and manifold wisdom that we mediate.

God Himself has come alongside us in His Son and Spirit, offering forgiveness to us all at His own cost, and even pleading with us to accept it. And He brings forgiveness to us, not that He may see the last of us, but make a new beginning with us in the fellowship of His own life which has no limit and no end. And we are in that fellowship in all its outreach and sweep to exhibit to men a love which saves us not because we are good, but that we may be made good, a salvation which is not self grown but God-given, which is not by our effort but by His Grace, with our consent.

No wonder that with such a message in their hearts J. P. Struthers of Greenock and his friend, A. D. Grant—those men of the Knotted Heart—would hail each other as they met on their way to their respective pulpits with the greeting : " Now stand we on the top of golden hours."

Mediation Through the Texture of our Experience.— We mediate this grace and truth, too, through the texture of our experience. For the Christian faith is both historic and super-historic. We do not disparage the use of the historic imagination in our appreciation of our faith, but there is more intimate approach to it than that.

The Romance of the Gospel is not a romance twice removed ; it is a romance re-enacted.

Dr. Denny used to say that the disciples never merely remembered Jesus, they experienced Him. They spent no time lamenting His absence, they were too intent on celebrating His presence.

When George Stephenson invented the locomotive he made it to function apart from himself, but the One who is grace and truth functions livingly in all the instruments He uses.

In preaching Christ, Christ is preaching through us. He lives again in every true utterance we make of Him. We never speak of Him in His absence, but always in His presence, whenever we speak reverently of Him.

We are not like the booking clerk at Cook's who hands out tickets to glorious landscapes and mountain heights he never sees and never climbs.

We are not like a banker who across a counter merely rings the changes of coins he does not own.

No, the context of the grace and truth of Christ is in the texture of our personal experience. Christ's redeeming Gospel has its testimony in our forgiven consciousness.

The first Covenant may have been mediated by the voice of a trumpet and the sound of words. The second Covenant has a more intimate and tender medium in the relieved anguish of the pardoned heart.

It is this that makes it possible to say more, for one has something to show. This Gospel has done something for us, and so can do something for others as we mediate it. And much that is in it breaks through language and escapes, but it is not lost; it is the truest exhalation of experienced grace and truth.

Mediation Through Worth of Character.—Mediation, too, must be through the worth of character grace and truth create. It lives in its creations—not in its reiterations. " Truth which has done little or nothing for us, cannot as coming from our lips, do much for others," says Dr. Denney.

Emerson's words about Cicero are very searching. He said : " In his writing there are many true and beautiful things, if only we had had the right to say them."

It is this want of worth in our character which leads to such want of weight in our speech. Remissness here means always poor transmission and feeble mediation.

Our hearers easily let themselves off from the challenge of the truth if we let ourselves off easily where its personal demands are concerned. It is so fatally easy to do what the short-sighted New York editor is said to have done—Rubbed out with his nose what he wrote with his pen.

This ministry of mediation is essentially sacramental. We bring the powers of one world to bear upon another, redressing the balance of the old world by bringing in the new.

And always the Infinite and Invisible must give evidence of themselves and be seen to be in play.

" Cut out any square inch of one of Turner's skies," Ruskin said, " and you would get the infinite."

From every street corner in Geneva you get a view of the towering heights of Mount Blanc. So in every simple deed and in the most routine duties of every day we are to bring the infinite into suggestion.

It has been said that in the Old Testament God had a temple for His people; in the New Testament God has His temple in His people. The God who inhabits eternity chooses these temples not made with hands as His manifestation point and as His agencies of mediation. And to be His temple is to recognise that what He claims we yield, what we yield He accepts, what He accepts He hallows, and what He hallows He uses in the mediation of His love.

Mediation Through the Wealth of our Thinking.—
We are also to mediate the truth through the clarity and wealth of our thinking. For experience of the truth offers no release from the responsibility of hard thinking about it. Thought and experience fertilise each other.

Bishop Gore used to urge ordinands never to forget the responsibilities of thought in the opportunities of service. We are to be interpreters of the truth as well as examples of it.

The coherence and congruity the Christian seeks in the truth as it is in Jesus is not the coherence of the schools, but that of the saints; not that of the philosophers but of worshippers. The world by its wisdom knew not God and never will.

Nevertheless, the Apostle speaks of a wisdom among the mature, and this wisdom is to be won by hard thinking wedded to deep experience of the living God. We all do far too little deep communing with the truth.

Abraham Lincoln, when he was postmaster and ordnance surveyor of the little town of Salem, used to sally forth in the morning with his letters under his hat and his ordnance instruments in his hand, and as he went—he says—he liked to get the north and south and east and west of an idea.

And here are dimensions of the truth we must survey if we are to comprehend with all saints its ranges. Our love is to abound more and more in discernment that we may discriminate between things that differ.

Many cleavages in the lives of Christian people and of the Church are due to our failure to distinguish things which differ. Many things are indispensable to Faith, like our documents, institutions, formulations and ordinances, and yet though near the centre are not the centre itself, and to treat them as all determinative may easily cut us off from one another.

As Dean Inge says, " Christianity has never divided in the chambers where good men meditate and pray; but they do divide so often by treating what is derivative as if it were the dynamic thing itself."

Deeper communion with the truth and clearer thinking about it, would greatly increase the effectiveness of our transmission.

Two Identifications Needed for Mediation.—In our ministry of mediation we can never ignore the receiving side of the activity. For we are not only to be Christ's men, but man's men too. The logic of the Incarnation must be honoured, and that involved a dual identification.

In the Word made flesh our Lord was God's word to man and man's word to God. Communion with the truth needs the common touch as its complement if there is to be any effective interpretation and mediation of its living content.

To stress for the moment and once again the first identification, we need to remind ourselves that the implications of Christian truth are endless, that half truths made to do duty for the whole truth are denuded of their organic force. Our Christian faith does not work in shreds and patches, but as a living whole. It is so perilous, too, to ignore the relation of Christian truth to all other truths as if we could separate one form of truth from another and receive them in different parts of our intelligence. The world of truth is one, and the nature of man is one, and attempts to conceive either as divisible is doomed to end in falsity and futility. We are always in danger of a hold up on one side or other of our ministration of the truths.

Dr. Leckie of Ibrox used to use one of the regulations of Ezekiel's ideal temple to press home this peril. It read : " He that entereth in by the north gate shall go out by the south, and he that entereth by the south gate shall go out by the north; every man shall go forth by the gate over against him."

That, he suggested, was not a mere regulation to prevent congestion ! It enshrined the principle of progression in the religious life. A man must not sit down or linger on that side of religion which first attracted him. His approach must be followed up by an appreciation of the complementary side. If he came in on the side of the emotional south, he must move toward the severer north of sound and clear intellectual appreciation of the truth.

Whether Dr. Leckie's exegesis was justified or not, his contention was, and our disposition to " rest and be thankful " at the wrong place, is the occasion of serious impairment in our mediation. There is an ancient saying I think to the effect that a man does not build his house on a bridge.

The Second Identification.—An African Chief is said to have represented this second side of our identification in the shrewd comment that when you go hunting ivory you find there is always an elephant attached.

There is always a human being at the other end of our task of mediation, and he has always to be regarded and reckoned with. And not infrequently the man at the other end has a complex.

Ezekiel in his call had to deal with such a situation. He was sent to a people who were harbouring prejudices and were perverse. It was not sufficient that he should have his vision and receive his commission; not enough either that he should assimilate the truth—eat the roll—before he attempted to disseminate it. He had to identify himself with his people as well as incorporate the truth. So we read that he got alongside— he sat where they sat. He tried to see things from their point of view; to get beneath their skin, so to speak. It seems, too, quite significant that there was a restraint of speech—a time lag— until he had allowed his gesture of sympathetic understanding to do its preparatory work. For with us speech must often wait until people have been given time to say things to themselves and let fall their barricade of self-defence.

The prophets later actions followed in the line of this double identification. As a Watchman he blew God's trumpet of warning, but as a sign or omen, he kept the common touch, lying on his side, rationing his food and drink, shaving his own head and beard, all in token of his sharing as well as showing his peoples sufferings and sorrows. It was with a heart-breaking sigh that he delivered his bad news.

The students at Cuddesdon under Edward King used to tell of the deep feeling their teacher showed when he reminded them of how Moses' anger flamed out against the sons of Aaron, Eleazar and Ithamar, " because they had burnt the son offering and not eaten it seeing it was given to them to bear the iniquity of the congregation."

It was as if the Ark which had to be borne on human shoulders had been committed against the instruction of Moses to the mechanism of a cart with wheels.

Interpretation must Facilitate Mediation.—Our mediation must be meaningful as well as purposeful.

To make it so, we need to get alongside and not stand over against men. To direct them to the Way, we must face the same direction, or their left will be our right, and their right our left.

This is the most demanding exercise any Christian man can undertake, but at all costs it must be fulfilled. Men who never open the Bible and who have no clue to the nature of Christian truth, are in a world of their own, largely apart from ours. Sometimes they say as much to us—that we live in another world than theirs, and it is as though we spoke a different language. And our mediation of the truth to them must make it " live " and must be intelligible.

In the task of getting the truth across to such, I often think of the way Helen Keller was brought out of her world of darkness and her living prison, for she was indeed one of " the spirits in prison." Miss Sullivan, her teacher, put Helen's hands under flowing water and then pressed into the palms of her hands the letters containing the formula for water, and so the little girl was able to put the two things together in her darkened mind.

We have that double office to perform—to bring unawakened souls under the living force of the truth in our personal life, and then when interest has been elicited, to link that living thing with its label in our speech.

Daniel Niles, in his challenging book *That We May Live*, which has just come into my hands, tells how some years ago when in the United States, he was invited to a theological school to address the students. Instead of addressing them he said, " You are learning to preach the Gospel ; I want you to preach the Gospel to me. Think of me as an American pagan who has never been to Church and never read the Bible. I have an elementary education, and am workman on the road."

The first thing the students said to him was—" You are a sinner," to which he replied, " What is that ? " Over and over again the retort was made—" I don't understand. Please use words that I know."

Unless men hear the message in the tongue they understand, what hope is there of our winning them for our Lord, and theirs ?

The Aim of our Mediation.—The aim of our mediation must always be kept clearly before our mind, and must determine all our approaches. The language barrier is not the only barrier. There is the barrier of our own reserve. Whilst irresponsible speech about the deepest things should be certifiable, we often make, as Cynthia Asquith remarks about herself, " Our reserve not a fortress but a prison, since the bars are on the wrong side." Or as G. K. Chesterton puts it, " We are so afraid of being taken in that we never are."

More than one who attended the Amsterdam Conference have referred to the unforgettable moment when Bishop Stephen Neill looking at that imposing gathering said, " When did you last try to lead someone to Jesus ? "

One who was present said that in his own heart that question created fears, for it had been so easy to be swept into positions of administrative responsibility with work on Committees and Councils, with days all full of preaching the Gospel from platforms and pulpit, that this first-hand form of personal dealing had become an experience of the past.

We all have to say things to ourselves about our own responsibility in this matter, and indeed it is only what we do say to ourselves about what is said to us that is really effectual.

We are not called upon to violate our natural disposition in our witness, but witness in suitable ways in both life and speech we must. All of us without exception are called to this office, and the power of God's spirit in our lives depends on our standing in with the truth as its sponsors, and delivering its message in intelligible ways to others.

The reported words of two negroes may sharpen the point as it presses on our own heart. " Lord help me," said one ; to whom the Lord replied, " How can I when you are doing nothing ? " And the other man put in the proviso, " Lord, use me, but in an advisory capacity."

The art in witness seems to be in what was once said of Sir Walter Raleigh, the distinguished Professor of Literature—" When he was talking to you, he always made conversation seem like collaboration."

The Measure of Our Mediation.—A supremely important consideration is the measure of our mediation. The gauge of it is so determinative both in our personal and corporal life.

Some of us have a very vivid recollection of an address Dr. Ferrier Hulme gave at the Leicester Conference in the Ministerial Session on the significance of the New Testament word " Kata "

—according to. The word represented the gauge set on the Divine side, and on the human side in the mediated grace of God.

On the side of God the references to God's overflow toward us are many, and all suggestive of an unlimited bounty of bestowment. It is called " the riches of His Grace "—His full and generous overflowing towards us (Phillips). It is grace given to us according to " the rich diversity of Christ's giving." It represents an overflow of power to us, the measure of which is beyond what any of us dare think of or imagine. Its measure is the power that wrought in Christ when He was raised from the dead; a power, too, able to subdue all things to its own purpose.

On our side the gauge is " according to our faith "—our capacity of appreciation and reception. And it is on our side where He set limits to the full and generous overflowing grace of God. It is able to subdue all things to its purposes—if we will let it. It will quicken our dead spirits into newness of life if we leave it room to operate. It will work in all the diverse ways in which our Lord's own ministry was exercised if we give it the chance.

A vital consideration, however, is that it will work according to the law of the Spirit of Life in Christ Jesus, and we must honour the law of it if we are to mediate the power of it.

And the Spirit of Life in Christ Jesus not only brings deliverance and buoyancy and the assurance of sonship and heirship, it is a life with an outreach in it which must needs find in our personal and corporate life the widest range for its expansion and effectual working.

We must never narrow the gauge.

The Tests of Effective Mediation.—The tests of effective mediation can be readily seen as we recall the thing " in character " with the Life which is seeking to subdue all things to its purpose. For what is essential in that life must " out."

One characteristic is a flowering piety—and it must be of the flowering and fragrant sort.

Few pictures are more graphic than that which Paul gives us of our Lord leading His people on His own triumphant way, spreading abroad His knowledge as we go, like a lovely perfume. And not a small measure of the triumph lies in the shedding forth of the fragrance. For fragrance and beauty are always witnessing and winning things.

Dr. Jowett used to tell of taking his morning walk through a New York park and turning round at a certain point every day about a clump of bushes. He took no notice of them, nor cared to stoop down and read their botanical description, till one Spring day he found them in full bloom and fragrance. And then he was intensely interested to discover the name.

Gandhi was once asked by a company of missionaries if he could give them any guidance about their propagation of Christ's truth in India. He is said to have replied that if he had had a hand in writing the New Testament, he would not have written ' Faith cometh by hearing," but " Faith cometh by fragrance."

Then as deed and speech are life's complementary forms of expression, and as deed and speech together were " the Life's own witness," the full range of these are called for if mediation is to be effective. Life's precipitates are in both, but not in both equally. And none of us can lay down the law for each other. The deed generally is prior and primal. We must win our right to speech. Most of us were won for Christ before a word was spoken. And when words of witness are given they should " distil as the dew." Witness that gives the impression of being forced is worse than silence. But when—as with the fall of dew—precipitation point is reached, as it should when men live in intimate communion with the truth, the word of witness must not be withheld.

Things which Impair Mediation.—Over and above the many things already named which impair mediation, I may mention *sombreness*. Nothing is so likely to obstruct the channels of grace as ungraciousness.

Isabel Cameron's " Doctor "—Robert Cowan of Elgin—told his people at his induction that he intended to hang his preaching gown on a sunbeam. Radiancy is " in character " always, and as airmen on landing make " a beam approach," so must we.

Then if a true spirituality—which is not a side of life but the whole of it—is an undispensable condition, it is also too sadly true that a *spurious spirituality* may be a serious impairment to mediation. Our interests must be as wide as life itself. Grace needs a full rich nature even as nature needs a full rich grace.

Dora Greenwell used to say that an isolated spirituality exhausts the soil that receives it, and spirituality needed constant contact with common life.

In George Herbert's vicarage garden at Bemerton a mulberry tree of many hundreds years old showed signs of languishing, but when it had grafted into it the branches of a thorn bush from the roadside, it revived and is blossoming still I suppose.

"Let me live in a house by the side of the road and be a friend to man" is a good prayer for each to offer.

Or to return, in conclusion, to the simile used in the beginning, of grace and truth instrumented through all the manuals of an organ.

Two defects are common, I suppose, in organs. One is ciphering, in which a key affected by damp keeps joining in when not called for on the score, and the other is when keys are mute and fail to vocalise the air which should be passing through the reeds.

The ciphering which impairs the rendering is the self which love fails to displace and dissipate ; and the keys which too often are void of music in us, are those which sound out the full rich praises of Him who has called us out of darkness with His marvellous light.

Our Commission in Retrospect

I am very sensible of the honour you do me in asking me to think aloud as I look back upon my ministerial commission.

There is a real value in reflecting anti-clockwise on the years which lie behind.

One of Rabbi Duncan's favourite ideas was that as in nature " day unto day uttered speech," so in life and Providence one day is speaking to another. One's latter days have their " say " in respect of former ones.

And one of the privileges of growing older is that one is allowed greater liberty in becoming reminiscent—though as it is said " reminiscences may easily become reminuisances," and the comment was made about Wordsworth that he became reiterative as he ceased to be creative.

We older folks like the Aberdonians hugely enjoy the jokes passed upon us ; like that of the boy on the village green who, having broken his cricket bat, approached the aged vicar for the loan of one, because he had heard his father say only the day before, that he had bats in his belfry.

Crossing the dead line, however, is never simply a matter of the calendar. We cross it when we cease to learn when we go out of training ; when we rest on our laurels—as someone said of another—" Don't you think his laurels are faded ? " and received the reply, " How else could they be otherwise, he's resting on them."

When Lord Palmerston was asked when he thought a man ought to be at his best, he replied, " At seventy-eight I should think ; I'm sorry I'm somewhat past it. I'm seventy-nine."

What one has to say will necessarily take somewhat the form of a personal narrative, though it need not be much the worse for that. I have always felt the fascination of the red streak in anything, though I naturally prefer the other fellow to show it.

God has His way of individuating His manifestations of Himself through personal lives, and as Shelley reminds us—

" Life like a dome of many coloured glass stains the white radiance of eternity."

The Personal Factor.—The abstract and the abstruse are never too alluring, and the personal provides a welcome relief.

An eccentric don in Oxford is reported to have taken hold of one of his pupils on the street and said—" Tell your father from me that one of the greatest evils of our time is the worship of abstract ideas. Good morning."

Truth takes a great hold on us when we personalise it, even places do when we personalise them, as was the case with Robert Hall.

When asked what he thought of Cambridge, he said " Very interesting place ; the place where Bacon, Barrowe and Newton studied and where Jeremy Taylor was born cannot but be interesting." " But," said his questioner, " What of the scenery ? " " O, very flat, a dismally flat country," was his reply.

Dr. Denney gives us a needful reminder, however, of four kinds of personal narrations. " When a man speaks to himself in the presence of God, as the Psalmist does, he is interesting ; when a man thinks about himself in his relation to God, as Augustine does, he is interesting ; when a man recounts God's dealings with him, as Bunyan does, he is interesting too ; but when a man thinks towards himself and speaks of himself, he is a ' bore.' "

How we all feel that the Apostle Paul could never be too personal in his epistles ; how we love to look into that great man's heart and read its secret there.

How we wish, too, that great men like Forsyth had not been so reticent about their spiritual history. And Forsyth was reticent even to his closest friends. He leaves whole areas of his spiritual development a gap. " Starting out as a liberal of the liberals in his theology, concerning himself with the Incarnation rather than the Atonement, he emerges as a believer and thinker, anticipating Barth, Brunner and Niebuhr—a right-about face."

The change was evidently gradual and took place during his London ministry, between 1880 and 1885. He came to see, by what process we do not know, that Theological Liberation led to a dead end, and that—as a recent essayist has reminded us—

only a Biblical Pauline faith contained an adequate interpretation of life, and a balm for the wounds of sinning man. But in all this I am comparing great things with small.

My Itinerancy.—My itinerancy of half a century has been evenly divided between Scotland and England, which seems to belong to the nature of things, since I am of Scottish parentage but have been brought up in England.

I seemed to have spent the years crossing and re-crossing the Tweed. I have sometimes stopped in my car at Carter Bar with the hood in one country and the back in another, and have stopped for quite a while wondering what part of me was Scottish and what part was English, and which was the better part.

I learned early to appreciate the fine opportunity given by Scottish Methodism to a raw youth. The high regard paid to the ministry, and the opportunity of concentrating one's energies within a limited area, together with the appreciation of Scotsmen for expository preaching, drew the best out of one.

A ministry in Scotland gives one the best possible chance of "being most in the main things." Besides, the Methodist witness in Scotland has had a deeper and wider influence on Scottish life than our numbers would ever suggest.

Devotion on the part of the Scot to his Church and minister are outstanding traits.

One soon learned to disregard the libel cast upon him that he was mean in the disposal of his money—such as that suggested by the story of a lady in New York who, presenting a collection box to a kiltie, pointed out the caption—" Give till it hurts," and receiving the reply after a prolonged pause—" Why the very idea hurts."

I have enjoyed every bit of my ministry both in England and Scotland, though I am left with the feeling, perhaps fictitious, that for the Scottish ministry there is more to show in things of a spiritual kind.

This may suffice, perhaps, believing as I do most fervently in the principle of " cross fertilisation " even where a minister is concerned.

I may add that I am Scot enough to wish that a dozen more Scottish Psalms and Paraphrases had been included in our hymnal, and English enough to wish that on some occasions we in Scotland quickened sometimes the tempo of our singing.

The Divine Imperative.—I am profoundly grateful that I have carried with me undiminished through the years the sense of the Divine imperative, and believe my sense of vocation is stronger than ever it was.

And as in the science of hydraulics, pressure is transformed into momentum, so the Divine imperative has primed my spirit with its initiative unfailingly. In small measure I have felt what greater spirits have known, that I was marching with destiny ; that when God makes anything or purposes anything, He puts his rhythm into it, which it is our privilege to pick up. And we are His poems embodying His thought and expressing His passion, and are created in Christ Jesus to take a certain path and to fulfil a certain part ; and that on that preordained path we share in the vibrancy and resiliency and exhilaration of God's own heart ; that as when He made the world at first, the morning stars sang together and the sons of God shouted for joy, so in our smaller world of human experience when we respond to His will—as the gold leaf to the electric charge—there echoes within us that which makes all life within and without symphonic.

In such answering loyalty, we experience what Handley Moule calls " the buoyancy of the believing heart."

It continues to be my faith and in part, my experience, that in every conjunction of circumstance there are three factors, not two. There is not only the event and the man, but God, and God not inert or static, but the prime mover in the situation, the living God moving on to fulfil His own holy and saving purposes.

And leaving room for Him, as He in His infinite condescension and courtesy leaves room for us, He upbears us and fills His part, making our own spirits the sharers of the beat of His own symphonic heart.

If there is any more thrilling experience in life than this, I have yet to know it.

To be caught up into a purpose other and higher than our own, is Life indeed.

The Divine Imperative Conjoined with Something Else. — This sense of a Divine imperative — which has strengthened and speeded me, has been conditioned by and conjoined with three things.

The first is an almost intimidating sense of one's ineptitude, incapacity and inadequacy. I have never felt equal to the task. Over and over again I have quoted to myself the lines of George Herbert which Susannah Wesley made her own :

> Only since God doth often make
> Of lowly matter for high uses meet
> I lay me at His feet,
> There will I lie until my Master seek
> For some poor stuff whereon to show His skill,
> Then is my time.

With the Apostle one has often exclaimed—particularly when facing sometimes a crowd and sometimes an empty space at an open-air meeting—" Who is sufficient for these things." And also that other great word of his, " We received the sentence of death in ourselves that we should not trust in ourselves, but in God that raiseth the dead."

Or, " That your faith should not stand in the wisdom of men, but in the power of God."

And, paradoxically enough, the sense of inadequacy has not only yielded embarrassment but enrichment, since it has left the greater room for God and tossed me to His breast.

It has also left room for what one might call " The blessing of the crossed hands "—the blessing of the unexpected and the unpredictable ; the blessing which was transverse because it fell out of the natural order and was taken up by the supernatural.

How often the minus on the horizontal plane has been transformed into a plus by the coming in of the vertical.

One's weakness has left room for God's surprise. One could sing with Miss Waring :

> Glory to Thee for strength withheld,
> For want and weakness known ;
> For the fear which sends me to Thyself,
> For what is most my own.

The Imperative Conjoined with Ignorance.—And then the sense of the divine imperative has been conditioned by and conjoined with a deepening and humbling sense of one's ignorance.

I am full of admiration of my brethren's powers and knowledge—which are my own blind spot. And I suppose it is true, as someone has said, that our blind spots lie side by side with our insights.

I feel this most in the presence of my brethren when they disclose their distinguished linguistic gifts, or when I go into a library and see staring before me how much I do not know. One has the oppressive sense of being a fraudulent person when amongst brethren who know so much and in libraries where so much lore is stored.

As I have travelled, I could put all I know about certain things into a matchbox, and even then the matches wouldn't strike. I could put all I know of science and mathematics into a small attache case. I might need a handbag on the rack to put what I have learned of philosophy and theology ; whereas I might need a few portmanteaux and a case or two in the luggage van to accommodate what I have learnt concerning things nearest to life in the realm of biography and autobiography.

One thing I have tried to do, which those who know me best will allow : I have tried to put a big " L " in my study, and have been glad to sit at the feet of my brethren when they have—I won't say aired their knowledge, but—let me in to the treasures of their minds.

I early formed, too, the habit of note-taking, which I have kept up unfailingly during these fifty years. It is a habit which my friends joke with me about quite frequently. They say I will be found dead with a pen in my hand.

One good friend enquired of his fellows in my presence, after a visit to Palestine, whether they had heard the report that several ink blots had been found on the walls by the Jaffa gates in Jerusalem. When the company said they had not heard of the report, he remarked, " But you do know that Ferguson was there lately."

The Imperative and Indebtedness.—This divine imperative has, however, been also conjoined with a deep and deepening sense of personal indebtedness.

Dr. Forsyth suggests that the Englishman is inclined to move about the universe with the pomp and swagger of one who says, " I am creditor to all men " as compared with Paul, " I am a debtor." Or as Samuel Rutherford says, " God's drowned debtor." I feel like that.

Amiel says that the indispensable conditions of great living are : a great cause to serve, and a circle of intimate friends to sustain one.

I have been favoured in having both.

I feel like a member of a prosperous Joint Stock Company, making small investments myself and receiving back large dividends not subject to tax, save that which arises from the sense that I have so little to give back in return.

I often quote to myself, however, in encouragement, the great words of G. K. Chesterton in his comment on St. Francis : " It is the highest and holiest of the paradoxes that the man who really feels he cannot pay his debt will be for ever paying it."

I found early the kind of idealistic friendship of which Browning sings :

> I crossed a moor with a name of its own
>   And a certain use in the world, no doubt ;
> But one hand-breadth of it shines alone
>   Mid the wild waste round about,
> For there I plucked from the heather,
>   And there I put into my breast
> A feather, an eagle's feather,
>   Well ! I forget the rest.

And what Frances Thompson found in Mrs Maynell I have found in " honourable women not a few," and like her, I dedicate any little thing I have done, to them.

> If the rose in meek duty
>   May dedicate humbly
> To her growers the beauty
>   Wherewith she is dowered,
> To you, O dear givers,
>   I give, too, your giving.

I salute in my spirit the friends who have been a comfort to me—in the double sense a paracletis and a paregoric.

Theological Trends.—One may fittingly preface a brief word about one's Teachers, Training and Technique, by reference to an outstanding trend in theological and philosophical thought.

Before the First World War Spiritual Monism was at its height. In the interests of the sovereignty of the rationalising intelligence, paradoxes and polarity in truth were all levelled down. Truth was made to do obeisance to a theory; the man was fitted to his clothes instead of the clothes to the man. Every sharp difference in religious experience was made to sacrifice itself to an interpretation of Reality in terms of Immanence. Men were engaged in trying to cast anchor within their own depths.

A very deadening influence was exerted by this theory on the spiritual life of the Church, and an arrest made on evangelistic activity.

But correctives were soon on the way.

The 1914-18 War revealed the deep-seated nature of sin in the heart of man. It could no longer be described as " a blundering quest after God "; it was seen to be a tragic perversity from which a man must be delivered.

In the realm of philosophy, Bergson made a distinctive contribution by presenting Reality as dynamic and Life impulses and intuitions as primal and prior to the rationalising mind.

Otto's influences in " The idea of the Holy " in the theological realm struck at the heart of subjectivism in religion and at sentimentalism in theology, making God central and not man. He showed religion to be autonomous and not a composite in the nature of man, and made " the numinous " the witness in man of the transcendent God.

The later emphasis by Buber on the essentially personal character of our relationship to God—in the " I and Thou " category, and not in the impersonal " I and It "—gave an additional momentum to the swing back towards a " truly evangelical theology," and the trend came round full circle.

The disposition of psychology, too, to treat prayer as auto-suggestion, and in Christian Science that God is " The All," received a decided setback.

The philosophical quest for unity in some ordered whole has had to rethink itself into the category of the dynamic and personal, rather than in the category of the static and abstractly rational.

My Teachers.—Of one's teachers, Peake, Denney, Forsyth, Otto, H. Macintosh, Oman, Temple and Maltby have wielded the largest influence.

Like the second named, I have had no use for a theology which would not evangelise. In many ways my teachers have helped to complement each other.

Peake held, as we know, to the mystical union of the Christian with Christ as the quintessence of the Pauline view. Denney held that the relationship was purely moral.

Peake used to say of Denney—whom he greatly admired— that what Denney saw, he saw with unmistakable clearness, but what he did not see, didn't exist for him at all. Peake himself found some writers " off his beat," and remarked about a certain Dr. Abbott, " His matches didn't strike on my box."

Oman in many ways complemented and corrected Otto. In administering correctives to Rationalising elements in religion, he felt that Otto had gone too far. The realm of the operation of " the numinous " was too exclusively in the feelings, and in emotional life as such there can be no true differentiations till they are lifted into the intellectual level of the value judgments.

On the other hand, Carnegie Simpson gently chided his colleague Oman for being so absorbed in conceiving what God is as to leave in some shadow what God had done.

William Temple, too, in one of his last letters, suggests a corrective he would himself make to his own contribution in theology to Christ as the Truth. He said he had viewed in terms that were too static the Logos, and had thought to present the consistency and coherence and completeness of the Logos as God's final Word in terms of a picture in which every part was present. He felt he would have been wiser to have rep- resented the Logos dynamically and to have presented the wholeness of Christian truth more in terms of a drama, in which the last act alone would crown the play.

Buber, Brunner, Farmer and Dodd have deeply impressed on one's heart and mind that personal categories are alone adequate to depict God's encounter with man in Judgment and Mercy, and that history must be envisaged as set in this pattern if it is to receive a truly Christian interpretation.

My Training.—My training, such as it has been, has been largely in the school of experience.

Laban's words to Jacob, " I have learned by experience," might indeed be my life's motto. Some, it is said, get their degrees by learning—most of us get our learning by degrees.

Experience is the College where we get the best of knowledge,
Though the price we have to pay is very high ;
For we find out to our sorrow, that the things we know
to-morrow
Are the very things we ought to know to-day.

The keeping of a student habit of mind and being ready to learn from everybody has been an invaluable aid in training.

The Yale men have a saying about the Harvard men that you can tell a Harvard man anywhere, but you can't tell him anything.

The years have brought their disciplines, and I am profoundly grateful they have been so mercifully light. The Greeks said " Pathemata Mathemata "—our sorrows have been our lessons.

Three things, among others, life has taught me :—

(1) That restraint plays as large a part in self realisation as does expression. Restraint has a major part to play in one's style and in one's attire, and it also goes into the schooling and ordering of the instincts and passions.

Self restraint is never the congenial occupation of youth, but it is not only the path to safety but to true fulfilment. For it is the law of any physical sensation when it has reached a certain height to turn into its opposite.

(2) That yielding to impatience in any difficult situation is always a mistake, and that to treat human perversity and obstinacy too seriously is a blunder, since the occasion of its expression is not in most cases very closely related to its cause, but rather the evidence of some emotional complex lying beneath it. A touch of kindly humour is the sure way out.

(3) That a disciplined adherence to the call of the Quiet Hour is indispensable to healthful Christian living and effective Christian service. Increasingly I feel the need and privilege of leaving God room to unveil His face and unfold His will.

My Techniques.—I have, like all my brethren, developed certain techniques which have served me well.

Believing with Jowett of Balliol that a large part of great living is to make the fullest use of our luminous hours, I have adopted what Marcus Dodd called " a pen and ink memory," and have never been content unless given insights have been recorded.

The notes have not always needed to be referred to, but by this habit they have been impressed on one's mind.

Being brought up in an area as a boy when the Manchester Canal was being cut, I seem always to have felt that I must cut channels between my reading and observation and my preaching.

Channel cutting has occupied quite a considerable part of my half century of ministry.

In administration I have believed deeply in letting patience have her perfect work. The peril of being in too great a hurry has often been impressed on my mind by two stories.

Phillip Brooks was once found by a friend pacing his study with impatient step, and when asked what was the matter, he said, " I'm in a hurry and God is not."

Dr. Hutton was once having his boots polished by a negro in America and showed himself rather restless as the black man disappeared out of sight to treat the boot heels. The man on his knees looked up and said thoughtfully, " We've even to give God time to get round."

An old Nannie in a Manse—so one of my old colleagues used to tell me—used to say, " God will never be late ; if He doesn't call when He's going, He'll call when He's coming back."

Finally, I have always made it my endeavour to make Pastoral visitation something more than a social call by meeting my people on the level of prayer in their homes. Indeed, I usually have said at the Reception Service that I craved this privilege for my own sake as well as for their own.

Musings on Our Messages
for 1953

Breaking the Complex. — How frequently " feeling the reproach of a situation " leads to a concern which becomes a constraint and ends in a commission.

The story of Nehemiah's call through the distress he felt about the broken-down walls of Jerusalem, is a good example of this; an even better example is Jonathan's heroic action— in company with his armour-bearer—assaulting the Philistines' garrison on the hillside on the strength of his faith that there was no restraint to the Lord to save by many or by few.

Saul and his people " in a strait " were in hiding; the same situation to a man of faith brought him " into the open."

How susceptible we all are in our finest hours to the reproach of the human situation : in which situation we are either part of the world's problem, or part of God's answer to it.

How susceptible we are, too, to any appeal to the heroic which is given to us.

To believe in a God of wonders surely should make us cry out, not " What is the world coming to ? " but " See what is coming to the world ! "

These hilltops held by the enemy were the very hilltops where Abraham received his promise of " the whole land."

Surely there is always a way out of any complex if any man feels a compunction about it—for such compunctions are not self-grown but God-given. We do not need in such cases to wait for a quorum before we act. We can always find some other as a kind of armour-bearer.

Any man can let God into a situation and free His action. Two are better than one, but no man needs to wait for another. The taking of the heights of Abraham and Scott's story of Ivanhoe both point the same way.

When we let God into any situation, as every one can, in commitment and prayer, we can be sure of three things :—

(1) That numbers, while they are something, are not everything. We can keep company with Gideon in whom the Spirit clothed himself, and set out.

(2) And there is no need to wait till everybody is ready, though a people prepared for the Lord is our greatest need. It is our prerogative to seize the initiative in the name of our God.

(3) We may find our way out of our complex, as often happens, by an unscheduled route.

Out of the Straits.—Another story of emergence from a strait place is that of the prophet's widow who was in a situation like ourselves, which makes us " cry out." She had an honourable name, and an honourable history, but that did not relieve her necessity or allay her fear that her house would be sold over her head and her sons taken into bondage.

We all of us—personally, and as a Church—come to an " end of ourselves " time, a wits-end corner.

Karl Barth said he was like a man climbing the winding stairs of a church steeple, when in the blackness and darkness of bewilderment he stretched out to steady himself and pulled the rope which set the bell ringing.

It is always a relief to know that faith is comforted despair, and that our own sense of inadequacy is an honourable condition. " Blessed be beggary " is one of the Beatitudes.

Robert Bruce, the author of some of the metrical Psalms, says that at one time he took hold of God with two fingers ; in a great time of need he was led to take hold of Him by his two hands.

It is part of God's purpose in our situation of desperate need to keep the clinging quality in our faith, and to render us continually His petitioners. He wants, however, to make us His partners, too. We can never be the chief party in our own relief, but we have a part to play in it nevertheless. We don't sit idly by looking at our fingers. We must bestir ourselves. " Borrow vessels not a few." Bring such gifts and powers as are ours into service. Make, too, our children a search party for us in the same task and engage their activity, since they are involved with us in the issue.

We are to commit ourselves adventurously in advance and in anticipation of the Divine action. The widow's action and that of her children would not pass muster as a step which mere prudence would commend.

Peter Mackenzie used to picture the neighbours tapping their foreheads ominously as the children went around borrowing the vessels, and saying to one another, " Her trouble has gone to her head, poor woman." But audacity is part of the children of God's outfit, and in story after story committal makes way for outlet.

Half-way through many a Christian procedure, we figure as " a spectacle to men and angels," but not finally ; and always the deliverance is on God's scale, not ours, and is a provision not only for immediate needs, but for future days

Our Quickening Ministry.—The failure of Gehani, wielding the prophet's staff, to raise the Shunammite's son and Elisha's success where his servant had failed, supplies many suggestions why we fail to quicken souls into life and the unfailing means by which it is done.

Ordinances and ritual observances can never be the substitutes for the prophetic spirit.

The prophet's staff—and the prophet's mantle—can never take the place of the imponderable factor which makes a prophet. The prophet's servant had all the orders needed and fulfilled all the ordinances, but " the child did not awake."

The truly sacred is never primarily in things or places, but in persons.

John Wesley's experience in Georgia bears that out. He was a fully ordained clergyman and utterly impotent as well.

Apparatus and appurtenances are not to be disparaged, but they need living hands to operate them. There is no breath in them. They need the plus to render them effective.

Neither is the mere perfunctory performance of religious duty of any quickening value. The northern farmer at Church " thought he said what he ought to 'av said—and come'd away." His prayer book was open at the right place and he knelt at the proper time—and that was that.

Neither are astuteness and cleverness of any avail in this kind of ministry. " Thou must be true thyself if thou the truth would'st teach." The reiterative is no substitute for the creative, and spiritual power is not operated through a deputy.

A Quickening Ministry lies in something that is suggested first by the closed door. None of us can live all our life in the public gaze. There must be periods of withdrawal when we are alone with God. And to shut out others is but the prelude to letting in God. How often we need to say with Abraham, " Tarry ye here while I go and worship."

We are wise to face our problem in the silence, and with the shut door. To walk to and fro before it as Elisha did, or to walk round about it as Nehemiah did, and Ezekiel did.

We then must link our human weakness with Almighty Power. We are never our bare selves, but all we can take hold of on the side of God.

We must always be ready to make the second identification as well as the first and get alongside ; mouth against mouth, eyes against eyes, hands against hands—and the miracle *does* take place.

Where the Children of this World are Wiser and can Give us Points.—Two principles of Jesus in his training of his disciples were :—

(1) That they were to learn from everything and from everyone—from flowers and birds and seeds, and also from doves and serpents and even from scoundrels.

(2) But they were to be discriminating in what they learnt, and were to follow the example, finally, of One only. " One is your Master."

We often slip up here in wanting to teach everybody and to learn from nobody. We become intolerant of other people's way of doing things—as the disciples were—and want to forbid them.

Jesus bids us learn from this rascal—the Unjust Steward—because he was a realist in two ways : (1) He was realistic in respect of two worlds. He saw clearly which was the collapsing world and which was the coming world ; (2) And he was a realist in his view of human nature. He had no illusions how he would be treated in the new world to which he was going unless he put his stake in it and made friendships in view of it.

(1) Life had found him out ; and as far as this world's craft was concerned, he had nothing new to learn. That world was falling about his ears and could never be built up again. He had fixed his cushion on a scaffolding which was now falling away from him. His only realistic action would be to act promptly and get away from it and make his fall as light as it could be made. His view of the world that was coming was realistic, too.

The prospect was drear indeed. His previous behaviour gave him no right to expect consideration there. So, realising that the time was short, he completely reversed his previous line of action. Instead of exploiting his master's tenants, he ingratiated himself into their favour.

He precipately transferred all his investments into " futures " because he saw that while he continued to have this holding in a falling market, this was going to be a total loss.

(2) His view of human nature, too, was realistic. He had no blind eye where people were concerned. He knew the motive which prompts men and he was ready for all the " moves " he knew they would make.

For us, too (1) the time is short; time is a decisive factor in our situation. Things never remain long as they are—never stay put in a Living Universe. We must not mistake the two worlds; the Coming World and the Going World. We must have clear views about which is the Life indeed. And we must act quickly. (2) Not, however, without taking men's full measure, anticipating their reactions and forecasting their next move.

Mohammed boasted of his knowledge of human nature, and decided not to ask too much from people.

Our Lord was more realistic. He knew better what was in man and asked everything. Even this scoundrel has this better sense of things, and went *outright*—the whole hog—in his decisive action to make friendships in the *Coming world*.

No cheese-paring action would content him.

Bearing the Ark on our Shoulders.—One of the most impressive addresses of Dr. G. G. Findlay was on the Parables of the Leaven and the Net, in which, on the one hand he spoke of the Leaven working from within outwards, gradually and secretly, and on the other hand of the Kingdom Net cast into the sea or the open waters and sweeping fish in by shoals.

The Operations of the Kingdom of God require both methods. The first method requires little or no organisation, but the second calls for special tackle, combined action, and the use of the proper bait and adequate appurtenances. The two methods are complementary and must not be set against each other.

At the moment I am thinking of an old injunction which properly indicates the relative places of personalities and organisations—the direction of Moses that the hangings and vestments of the Tabernacle might be borne on the six carts by oxen, but that the Ark itself was to be carried on human shoulders.

It is not an easy thing to decide just what things can be delegated to organisation and what cannot.

We can be sure, however, that the really sacred things of life which represent the Shekinah in us must not be so delegated. In a deep sense every man must bear his own burden—" the pain of being a man," the honouring burden of his responsibility for his life and service and his concern as a brother for his fellows.

There are no easements in respect of our obligation to fulfil the will of God to make the higher choice, to take the holy way. As Christophers, too, there is our burden of mediation—an honourable and honouring ministry indeed — to bear the altar of the mercy seat, the living manna, the wonder working rod, as well as the table of the Living Law. No one can gain release by relegating his personal burden of responsibility and choice to a Church or priestly order.

Montaigne once offered as Mayor to take the affairs of Bordeaux on his hands, but not on his heart—a practice some adopt in other realms.

One of the most tremendous facts of life is our inability to really divest ourselves of the intimately sacred in human life. When we are told we are victims of environment, we reply that we can choose the environment in which our true life is lived, and God has set eternity within man's heart.

God's way of dealing with us, too, is always fully personal.

Whether God commits to mechanism any part of His universe we do not know, but in dealing with us He deals with persons. He says, " I will bear and I will carry."

Our fitting response to God's honouring of us in our personal relation is to honour Him and others in the same way.

On Getting Kindling.—Our Lord's words about His coming to send fire on the earth is surely a promise to give to human spirits " kindling."

So Charles Wesley interpreted it we know. Ignition is life's supreme need. We need stability, but we get it through incentive even as a top finds equilibrium through momentum. We need kindling to undertake any task—both to set us off, and to keep us going. There are latent gifts and powers in us, too, which can only be released by flame. We readily become an infliction when we are uninspired. How often we cry out as did Christina Rossetti, " My faith burns low, my hope burns low," though mercifully we go on to her later verse, " Love's fire thou art, however cold I be."

T. R. Glover used to say there were times when he would not give a " Thank you " for a counsel, but would give almost anything for an inspiration.

It is in high or low ignition that Religions are to be judged. The God that answereth by fire is the God. If God has to be wakened from sleep or has gone on a journey, or is only to be approached by a select class—that religion does not fire our ardour. It is only a God who has done something for us we could not possibly do for ourselves who gives us kindling.

Life has many ignition points, and none of them are to be disparaged. Nature's beauty sets our spirit aflame though it fails us when we most need it, in hours of darkest grief, as it failed Sir Walter Scott.

Remembrance is a kindling flame ; while we muse the fire kindles. Human Fellowship is a kindling ministry. One loving heart sets another on fire.

Worship, too, brings the worlds together, as it did for the village blacksmith, and the two worlds are like flint and tinder to each other. But supremely, kindling comes through what Christ has brought—making God intelligible, available, revealing Him as always near and never disdainful of any of his children, and never willing to stand out of their sorrows and suffering and sin.

These three things always kindle : (1) That Christ is always ready to begin a friendship with us. (2) That He is willing to take us as we are and to begin with us where we are. (3) That He always begins with what we've got, however poor and mean it is.

On Keeping Up the Fires.—Three injunctions about the lights and fires of the ancient sanctuary have always seemed significant to me. They are full of suggestion about the place of worship in human life :—(1) The Sanctuary lights and fires were to be lit from within. No strange fire was to be brought from without; they were to be lit from one another. (2) Then when the priest was trimming the lamps, he was to keep sweet incense burning on the altar combining his simple duties with sacred ordinances. (3) And the fires on the Altar

G

were never to be allowed to go out. They were to be kept continually burning.

(1) The first suggests how central and constitutive a thing worship is in human life. The light of the sacred in us is not as some would have us believe, something brought in from without, by wishful thinking or priestcraft ; nor is it a composite of fear and fancy. It is God's central witness to Himself in our breast. In every heart God has set His own undying fire.

(2) Then worship, while it owes nothing to ourselves or others in its origin, must nevertheless be co-ordinated with life. We must not isolate it. The world eternal and the world of time and common duty are made for each other. They are sublimely complementary and fertilise each other. There is always the sacramental when the two conjoin. Life in all its order and service needs worship to keep it from going to pieces— it is a texture which needs the warp interwoven with the woof to give it consistency and strength.

(3) Then, these sacred fires of the Altar must be given fresh fuel continuously ; they must never be allowed to go out. Provision must be made perpetually for an office so constitutional to human nature as worship. Many fires will fade—youthful zest will go—the fires of passion die—but this fire must be preserved. How continually, wherever they went, did the patriarchs build an altar when they pitched their tents.

Continual worship is the only barrier against an invading worldliness, against unhallowed ventures, unauthorised programmes and unblessed friendships.

Can these Bones Live ?—Below a picture of the towers and spires of Oxford, Newman has these words written : " Can these bones live "

It is one of those questions " We breathe back again in prayer to Thee." It is the way of all institutions and organisations to lose the first impulse which gave them birth. They become exhausted of life. It is the same, too, of religious phrases. When they were first coined they were instinct with life, but they became in time soulless and dried.

Every living thing needs embodiment. It is not only true that " It takes a soul to move a body," it takes a body to incarnate a soul. We need a framework for living things. The peril, however, is that the institution which at first embodied the living idea in the end buries it and the two lie in death together.

But that need not be the end of the story. It is never God's intention that it shall be. God as always is in the initiative and speaks to prophetic souls and first bids them take to heart the reproach of the situation. Then they are to carry on with their prophetic functions even when it seems most hopeless. The first stirrings of life may be feeble. The first response may be in re-organisation—bone coming to bone and sinew to sinew. We must never despise organisation, but we must remember its limitations. The prophetic function must continue to be exercised. We do not say as the Quaker did to Wesley, " I will speak if the Spirit moves." We rather say, " I will preach that the Spirit may move." God calls for our co-ordination. The supreme moment of the prophetic movement is when the man of God becomes the prophet-priest—as indeed Ezekiel did when he prophesied to the four winds. Our great appeal is not to the situation in itself, nor to the life of man as we see it, but to the Life of the Spirit as we know it. Every man's highest privilege is to bring in God—the " Breath from the four winds." We can claim our share in the Life of the Spirit not only for ourselves, but for the dying cause.

And as Oxford, the home of lost causes, became through spiritually - quickened John Wesley, the base for a revived Church, so it may be once again. We may read the possibilities of the last Oxford Conference in the light of Ezekiel's story.

By These Things Men Live.—Hezekiah's summing-up of his experience after his recovery from his sickness is a worthwhile study. His hairbreadth escape from death and his endurance of the pangs of pain and of misgiving, and his eventual recovery through the mercy of God might easily have been differently described.

It is by these kind of struggles men generally say " they die " ; they succumb : rather they may set one man on his feet.

The King, however, had learned to ready history as HIS-STORY, and that made the difference. It was all part of a story which was serial in its character and the approach to the grave, and the return from it was part of the Divine plot.

When God is in anything and His activity is sensed there are treasures in the darkness, gain in seeming loss, and a far-off interest of tears, " Though not revealed to feeble sense our spirits feel Him near," and Life, not death, is emerging in the process. The struggle is like that of the chrysalis bursting its bonds, and of the bird breaking its shell and discovering its larger life.

All that the Ark symbolised is present in our experience of struggle and upheaval. There is mercy present and mystic sustenance, and the wonder working and transforming rod which quickens dead things into bloom.

Both we and the Church may come out of our life and death struggles enriched and with a new lease of life and power. What we said at the gates of the grave we take back. Like one ancient preacher, we look at life again and revise our judgment of it. And instead of the mourning note of the dove, there will be the praise of a man newly endowed with life.

The peril always is that by not integrating our struggle with the ever-living and energetic purpose of God, we die of that which in the divine intention would re-create and renew us.

Frances Ridley Havergal tells of her own learning to live by certain experiences of hers which she linked with Ezekiel 40. 4. " To the intent that I might show thee these things have I brought thee hither."

We can only see some things when our eyes are shaded, or in some depth, or darkness.

Surveying the Wondrous Cross.—How utterly fitting the word survey is. It suggests something which calls for more than a passing glance and something which has more dimensions than one, and which must therefore be viewed from many angles.

" My ransom and peace my surety He is." In it we get what Paul called " The measure of the gift of Christ." And that overwhelms the sight and search it engages. It suggests, too, the use of instruments of measurement. It is God's standard we are to honour, not our own. We bring to it a right sense of our accountability, and our sense of unworthiness and penitence —only so can we survey it.

It is a Wondrous Cross. That He of all the sons of men should be on it. I once heard Principal Macgregor link this wonder with the story of Asahel—swift as a young roe—lying dead on the roadway. And all that passed by stood still. Death and he made such a strange conjunction. And then he had not waited for death to reach him ; he had run into its arms.

The Second Wonder is that God who seemed so absent should be more there than in any other event in history. The little fellow in Richard Jefferies story said, " If God had been there, they wouldn't have done it."

But He was there, not opposite that dying figure, but alongside it.

The Third Wonder is that it is the place where so many divergent roads meet and opposites conjoin. " Judgment and mercy, sorrow and love." The friends of Job said to him they would show him the hand of God. God's hands as they saw them were punitive hands. As we see them they are wounded hands.

The Fourth Wonder is that it represents the great divide of the world—of human history and of our personal history. Paul's logic of the Cross and what it meant is " We thus judge . . . we which live should henceforth not live lives of our own." Here, if anywhere, men pour contempt on all their pride and yield up all they have claimed as their perquisites.

This is where we turn to find what God really is.

This is where we are called to make our abiding place.

This is where we really can give ourselves away, as Dick Sheppard—at his ordination—did, clasping a piece of paper on which was written " O love I give myself to Thee ; Thine only evermore to be."

Accepted in the Beloved.—Robertson Nicoll used to say this was the kind of text too little preached from. It is a haunting phrase, and one to take with us to the Sacrament and throughout life. For it is the key to which the music of the whole Christian life is set. From beginning to end we are " Dear for someone else's sake." We are accepted under the covering love of Another. It is a much more precious and a much less precarious way of acceptance than being received in our own right or on our own recognisances.

The reception of Mephibosheth at the royal table " For Jonathan's sake " is a fitting picture of ourselves. The " dead dog " was under no illusions as to the ground on which he placed his feet below David's table. I dare say David never saw the lame figure as he was ; he saw him lyrically and rapturously as Jonathan. Mephibosheth had not climbed into favour ; he had been sought out, and all the bounty he received he owed to Another. He was " accepted in the Beloved." Chosen not for good in me.

Elizabeth Barrett loved to tell how she—years older than Robert Browning, and an invalid—was found " rusting in a pool of tears," and how it was betwixt a mystery and a miracle that he ever turned his eyes her way.

This acceptance in the beloved is in the unqualified love God has for His only begotten Son, who said "Herein doth My Father love Me, because I lay down My Life for the sheep." In our unworthiness we might well fear the Father's heart would feel aversion to us were it not for this. We are only fit to be tossed to the crows—we feel sometimes.

There is nothing precarious either. The branch we pull down may spring upwards again and leave us in deprivation—but not this love-laden branch which by its own weight lies at our feet and within our reach.

It is this kind of acceptance which takes us off our self-centre. It is this kind of acceptance, too, which makes it possible to be " beautified in the Beloved."

Love the Condition of Manifestation.—Love is the condition both of manifestation and of mediation. Judas could not understand why our Lord could not broadcast His manifestations of Himself to all and sundry. He received a reply which told him that the most intimate manifestations can only take place under personal conditions in which love made communication possible.

I remember Bailie Gray used to delight in this truth. Music says " If you love me I will manifest myself." Nature in all its beauty and splendour says the same.

Art and Literature only give their treasures to lovers.

Bailie Gray used to tell of going into the Tate Gallery with an artist friend who pointed out the wonders of the paintings there. Some of them were worth £10,000. The Bailie did not want to dispute the point, but said he had seen grocers' calendars he liked better.

Supremely this is true in the realm of intimate personal relationships. We cannot confide to order. We need an affinity of spirit and the kindlings of affection before we can open out our heart to people.

It is God's design to make His abode with us, but He can only make His home where there is the outgoing of the heart.

It is well to remind ourselves that God is not passive in the situation. And He is not promiscuous either. He cannot be, and remain our personal God.

We may well ask how we can so love our Lord that He will make His unveiling to us.

Love cannot be commanded or coerced. But we can allow Christ's selfless love to woo and win us. We can open our hearts to His overtures and advances. We can let Him have His way and His sway in our hearts and will.

In this intimacy of Love, there will be an end of a certain kind of questioning. (There were two kinds our Lord referred to in the Upper Room.)

And there will also be an expanding appreciation of the unfolding mind and heart of our Lord.

The Gospel Lives by its Beautiful Things.—It is on such beautiful things as the breaking of the Alabaster Box that the Gospel lives. The woman might have used it for herself, but she broke it at the Master's feet and the story of her action became immortal. What we spend on ourselves has no second history.

The Moslem faith lives by the sword. The Confucian faith lives by the scroll. Our Christian faith lives by the spikenard poured forth.

Such beautiful things are of the essence of our Christian faith. Four things go to make it up : a profound sense of need ; a happy sense of deliverance ; an overwhelming sense of indebtedness ; and an ever present constraint to do something in return. And as " drops of grief can ne'er repay," the action called for is in some extravagance of committal and service.

How strangely enought broken things are beautiful. Most things are spoiled by being broken. Other things are fulfilled : the broken body—the broken and contrite heart—the broken alabaster box.

These beautiful things may be symbolised by material things, but their real beauty lies in their moral and spiritual sources. These are " the things of beauty which are a joy for ever."

These beautiful things by reason of the love they bear, have a significance which the doers never dream of. This woman doing what she could, did far more than she could have imagined. Our Lord would catch the fragrance of this spikenard in the garden and on the Cross. How poor a register our own consciousness is of what we do, when we act under the impulse of adoring love. Did Dorcas know all she did, or did Simon Peter realise that the sick were being healed in his shadow ?

These beautiful things on the one hand are our witness; on the other hand they judge us. This act took Judas Iscariot's measure and the measure of the disciples. People may be "sized up" into plus people and minus people—those ready to appreciate, and those ready to disparage. Little as we know it, we are all giving ourselves away.

Jesus put a plus on every simple offering—the widow's gift; the receiving of a prophet, and much else.

The timeliness of this beautiful thing and the originality of it and the courage of it, make it immortal.

Justified by Faith.—A special plea is made for the preaching of the great doctrines of our faith.

Martin Luther called this doctrine " The article of a standing or a falling Church." This is the grace wherein we stand.

When Dr. Dale told a friend he was going to preach a series of sermons on Christian doctrine, he received the discouraging reply, " They won't stand it." To which the Doctor replied, " They'll have to."

Silvester Horne tried to present this doctrine by saying it was God taking the will for the deed. But he proceeded to say it was not idle wish God took for the deed; nor was the deed ours, it was God's. The will, too, God took for the deed was the seminal principle in the deed which would follow in answer to God's own deed.

The deed on which all rests is that deed by which our Lord put away sin by the sacrifice of Himself.

In the light of the selfless love of Christ in dying for us, we all stand condemned; we have all come short. But by that same sacrificing Love we are offered full and free forgiveness—and to accept that forgiveness is to be justified.

By His Cross we are at once acquitted of past sin and accepted into God's favour.

Dr. Thomas Chalmers used to begin almost every day with what he called " an act of confidence " in Christ as his only sufficiency, and he used to remark, " Whatever should I do if God did not justify the ungodly. By Faith we leave room for Christ to fulfil His office as Saviour. We put our name, so to speak, to the dotted line made out for us in God's promise, and by so doing " set our seal that God is true." As we do, so God, who was once a desert to us and afterwards a Dread, becomes our Delight. We live in His favour and in the Father's lighted and protected and sacramental world.

The result is peace—the tranquilising of the soul. It is not self satisfaction, for all ground of boasting is gone.

God's way of justifying the ungodly by faith is the only way out from life's dead centre, and the only way in to cover and peace.

O God, Thou art My God.—Dora Greenwell's monogram on her books was " Et teneo, et teneor " (I hold and am held).

The Christian Life is best expressed in this double clasp and grasp. He will hold me fast and I must hold to Him in personal trust. It would be difficult to say more in six monosyllables than this : " O God, Thou art my God," and yet no man ought to say less. Man is not yet a full person till he has got this length, for part of the real life of every man lies in God. Alas, many never possess their possessions in Him.

This kind of knowledge is really knowledge of the Bible in the original—for Scripture is all begotten of personal relationships with God. They encounter Him and then became engaged to Him in life and purpose. The Bible was all lived before it was written.

The God we find in this personal way is the same God to everyone, and yet is not the same, since He is " my " God—a God to me in my particular tradition and with my particular temperament and need.

A father is the father of all his children, yet each knows the father in a distinctive way. There are no " dittos " in our life experience of God. God progressively becomes our God as life opens out to us, and as we open out our own life to Him. He becomes distinctly our God not by our easy acquiescence, but as in some emergency of experience and need, we welcome Him.

The Psalmist said God became known to him when " his sore ran in the night." Job had known God by the hearing of the ear till a crucial experience came when he said " Now mine eye seeth Thee."

Our experience of God may not be like Luther's or Wesley's —perhaps like Lydia's. But in every such experience of God we can say together, " He drew me and I followed on."

God becomes our God as we respond to His overtures. By the stirring of our heart to seek Him. For " the seekers are the next best sect to the finders," and all finders are seekers first.

We are encouraged in our search by the reminder that God's right hand sustains us. God makes Himself available.

And Thou Mayest Add Thereto.—Dr. W. L. Watkinson at the inauguration of the Twentieth Century Million Guineas Fund, preached on this text. I don't know anything he said, but it has a new significance for 1953.

As David laid his stores of gold and silver and iron for the building of the Temple at the feet of Solomon, it was with a catch in his voice he said, " And thou mayest add thereto," even as many now within the veil may have purposed to share with us in a great enterprise.

His tone, however, was not disgruntled as he realised that his limitation spelt another man's larger opportunity. He generously passed on what he had scoured the surrounding countries to secure, to his successor.

Appreciation for what has already been done is an indispensable preparation for what we are to do. The old men's vision must fertilise the young men's dreams. No one can make history who does not appreciate history. As Denney says, " If you take out of what is, what was, what's left ? "

What Paul has contributed, and Luther and Wesley, are part of our stock-in-trade in this high enterprise. But they, without us, cannot reach fulfilment. Every person and every generation are needed for the erection of God's Temple on the earth.

There is a great principle of continuity and of community in all God's work. One man is no man. A cross section of history is no history at all. Fragmentation in that realm is false and futile. " A thing is what it is becoming " and is " what it does," but the operations of life are continuous and cannot be pin-pricked as you might pin-prick a moth for exhibition.

Our vital question is what we can add. We can devote the iron of our sinew and strength, for there are three stages in any enterprise—the onset, the grip, and the drag—and stamina is an indispensable requisite in the service of a cause.

Alfred Tucker and Howard Somerville realised this and so did Alexander Mackay.

We can contribute the silver of our intelligence. God can use our mental alertness. He is embarrassed by our confused thinking. Moses called on Hobab to come with them that they might do him good, but his father-in-law did not fall for this bait. He asked him to be their intelligence officer, and that was successful.

We can give, supremely, the gold of our love and our allegiance. We have made no real gift to the Divine enterprise if we have put our love under any reserve.

When Joan of Arc was asked how she always won success, she said she did not know, except that perhaps it was that wherever her flag went, she went with it and stood under it.

Fellow Helpers to the Truth.—Much is being said, and rightly said, about the restatement of the truth. An ever greater need is the release of the truth and its fuller experience in the common stuff of living. The greater need is for the reality of the truth to be borne out, not in literary form merely, but in veritable practice. The truth as it is in Jesus meets need as it is in life, but the two need to be brought together, and truth's inherent power manifested.

Truth always needs a base.

We lost Greece in the last World War not because of lack of planes, but of aerodromes. The landing places and fuelling bases were wanting. And truth always lands on a personal base, and sets out from one. In dealing with men our Lord always landed there.

Where truth fails is always in the absence of whole-hearted adherents who are its fellow helpers. Columbus said he could have done much more if only his crew had been whole-hearted in the enterprise, and had been less of hirelings in spirit.

Our best witness to the truth as fellow helpers of it, is to live in the truth and on it ; walking in it, incorporating it into the swing of our very movements ; making our whole life march onwards to its rhythm. For the truth is quick and powerful and seminal. It fertilises our virtues, reinforces our courage ; it is our element, and our larger freedom. And as the truth bestows its inspirations and incentives, it asks to be borne by us and beyond us.

It asks not only our communion but our communication.

We are like Paul to be its chosen vessels, to bear Christ's name and nature to men.

Of the parson in the *Deserted Village* Goldsmith said, " Truth from his lips prevailed with double sway, and fools who came to scoff remained to pray."

We can become fellow helpers to the truth by welcoming the fellowship of others engaged in advancing the same cause.

By standing ourselves unreservedly beneath the banner " given for the display of the truth," making our life its flagstaff. And by setting up signs that all the world may see—signs of the King's presence, victory signs of His triumph, and irresistible proofs of His transforming power.

By this shall all men know that we are His disciples. And by such evidence the world may believe.

The Art and Value of Repetition.—The Apostle was not apologetic when he said the same things over again. It wasn't grievous to him and it was salutary for his hearers.

As Dr. Johnson affirmed, " We need to be reminded more than to be informed."

A Puritan has it that we are so dull to perceive, so prone to forget, and so slow to perform, that the truth needs constantly to be repeated to us.

James Smethan said he never saw anything at first, he always seemed to wake up to it—man of gifts and artist though he was.

And when we see things, we only at first see them in fragments of their meaning ; we do not see them in all their relationships, or see the whole. And to see things really, we must get them in focus and see them in perspective and proportion.

Our great peril is that we gain a superficial familiarity with great Christian words and phrases without ever sounding their depths. Not only are we to possess truth, truth is to possess us.

The first tap of the hammer does not drive the nail home, and the words of the wise are to be as nails fastened in a sure place—not in the memory only but in the texture of our life.

How prone we are to forget is often referred to in a dozen or more hymns we could quote : " I forget so soon, the early dew of morning has passed away at noon."

The book of Deuteronomy, by its very name, suggests the necessity of recapitulation. The Apostle said Christian people needed to be reminded to " Rejoice." So many find security in the Gospel who never discover exhilaration in it. They do not live happily in its inspirations.

We are all slow to perform. How few of us allow truth to run its full circle?

John Newton's slow discovery of the iniquity of the slave traffic is an instance. But we can supply equally impressive examples of it in our own practice. Our blind spots lie side by side with our insights. A man is blessed in his deeds. No man can think himself into the Kingdom of God. How tremendously we need practising Christians.

A pupil of Madame Schumann's who practised five hours a day said she began to feel exhilaration about the third hour.

We are inclined to become impatient when things are repeated as Isaiah's hearers were. "Whom will he teach knowledge?"

But, line upon line, here a little, there a little, is the order, and all repetitions are not vain.

And in our treatment of ourselves the patient must minister to himself. "The medicine as before" is often the prescription we most need, for our malady is generally of the chronic kind.

When the subject of depression, the Psalmist asked himself again and again, "Why he was cast down," since God was always there to be the strength of his heart.

It is Consent Makes the Match.—Thomas Goodwin, I think it was, who used the story of the wooing of Rebecca to press the claim of the Gospel that it is consent makes the match.

"The soul of man may be sick with desire for the beloved, but it is its choice that starts it on its way to meet the Bridegroom. All that long journey of a thousand miles might have ended in nothing, all those wedding gifts have remained unworn, and all Eleazar's pleading have been of no avail, if the maid had not given her consent. It was not Abraham's faith and foresight, not Isaac's princely presents, not Eleazar's passionate pleading, not all of them together that made the match. It was when Rebecca said 'I will go' that the match was made."

And so it is with the match between our Lord and ourselves. We may have good desires and never act on them—like a man coming to cross a river only "thinking it over"—or a farmer with a field to plough only "turning it over in his mind."

This resting short in desire without committing ourselves, is like trying to dig without a spade; like attempting to sail without a ship; like trying to fly without wings; like trying to build without material, and like fighting in fancy without a weapon.

To stop short of consent is to let everything come to nothing.

Many things lead up to consent—and it is consent not assent that is in question. An unexpected meeting may do it at the crossroads.

Moses, Saul, Florence Nightingale, Caroline Oliphant, Augustine, all came to crossroads.

When desire mates itself with choice, then consent makes the match.

Myriads desire the better life, but their desire remains unmated, and so nothing comes of it.

In choice there must always be the elimination of something. We can't have it every way. And often one desire excludes another—they stand opposed, and to choose one means the rejection of the other.

The objects of desire stand in a certain succession—and what is prior is decisive.

Getting the Truth Across.—Getting the truth across, especially to the outsider, is often our greatest problem. Making the two identifications with the truth and with our constituency, and choosing the right medium in understandable language, is our hardest lesson, only to be learnt by the method of trial and error.

Perhaps one or two actual experiences on this line may give some kind of a clue.

Yesterday, with three other ministers in a Church's Campaign, we went to a large paper works employing a few thousand employees. The management was sympathetic to our effort and gave twenty different sections of the works half-an-hour off during the working hours to listen to us.

We worked in pairs. One minister gave a five minutes' introduction, the other a ten minute talk, and the remainder of the half hour was given over to questions and answers.

Our first assignment was to a company of about fifty girls between the ages of seventeen to thirty.

My colleague, a Baptist minister, introduced, and I gave the talk.

I opened by remarking upon the delight and interest of early years, and told the story of a Highland maid who was advised to go to the doctor by her mistress, as she was not looking well. On her return her mistress asked her what the doctor had said.

" He told me," said the rather simple girl, " that I had youth on my side, but he didn't give me anything for it."

This led on, after the interchange of a few smiles, to a talk on how youth did not continue to be " on our side." Life's choices and friendships lay before us, and responsibilities came. The life of time and sense tended, as the years wore on, to form a vicious circle, and exhaust itself.

Here, a story of what formed a vicious circle, came in usefully. A boy coming from the chemist's was carrying a bottle of cod liver oil. A gentleman meeting him asked if he drank it himself. Yes, and his mother gave him sixpence for every bottle he drank. " You must be quite well off, then. What do you do with the money?" " Oh !" said the boy, " mother uses it to buy more cod liver oil."

The pleasantry made it possible to get home the point that all sensations of pleasure tend to move in circles which narrow and afford less and less satisfaction—indeed change into their opposite—and that God had set eternity in our heart, and only as we honoured His purpose could life reach its true fulfilment.

Christ offered Life with a Capital " L." He alone can break up life's vicious circles.

Our next assignment was to a mixed company of men and women ages ranging from thirty to sixty. They were all squatted on the retiring room floor around us.

The talk on this occasion was on how our personal relationships determined so much in life, far more than our material circumstances.

In business, in marriage, and in almost every realm, these were the chief factors. And in so many instances these relationships had broken down, and needed to be restored. The personal relationship with God was the most vital in life, and this had been broken down by our sin and pride, but Christ came to restore these relationships, and offered the restoration to men now. The point was stressed that on every occasion in His intercourse with men our Lord landed on the personal issue.

In other assignments where machinery was in motion, we spoke of the first necessity in coming to a machine was to enquire how it worked ; what was the designers' plan, and what was the nature of the work intended. This led naturally to a talk on " It is He that hath made us, and not we ourselves," and

God's design and purpose should be our first and not our last concern.

Later talks with little groups found their clue in the fact that some of the paper made in the works was water-marked, and was used for cheques and bank-note purposes.

This led us to ask how many factors went to make up life. Some said two—the man and the event. No; life has three factors—the man, the event, and God. Water-marked in life was God's own signature of His presence and purpose.

Recently at a High School in the Campaign, with the headmaster presiding and with 300 young people of the teen age present, the talk was on Christ's claim, " I have the keys."

It might have seemed to the prisoner who heard the words that the warder had the keys, or that Imperial Caesar had them. But no. Our politicians and scientists often make claims to have the keys. But the politicians have only the keys of the cupboard, and the scientists have not the key to the Temple of Peace on their girdle.

Christ has the keys of the future—our own future and of the world's future. Fate and chance and luck have not. Christ has the keys of our freedom. The prisoner on Patmos was bound in body, but he was in the Spirit on the Lord's Day. Whom the Son makes free they are free indeed. Christ has the keys of fulfilment, both in our personal life and in the life of the world.

The chorus in the book the prisoner wrote was " King of Kings and Lord of Lords."

A seeming anti-climax in a succeeding chapter represents this Christ with the keys standing before a closed door. He will not force the door into our own personal life. We have the key of that door, and all our future and freedom and fulfilment calls on us to " Let Him in."

The Value of Biography to the Student and the Preacher

MAN is so made—with blood in his veins and not water—that he turns as by an instinct to the coloured rather than the plain. His preferences lie strongly towards that which bears in it the blood-streak of experience. And he loves that literature best which is dyed red with the warm blood of life. Such predilections do man credit; they are neither unwholesome nor unwarrantable; they answer to something deeply embedded in his very texture. For when the Master of our being wishes to carry a point with us, though He suggests and supports His end and aim in the secondary and supplementary region which bears the cast of the "philosophically pale," He exerts His greater pressure in the warm pulses of living action and experience. And just as by some necessity of his being, isolated ideas lose meaning for man, and disconnected facts fail to grip his mind, so in literature what is non-personal or anonymous seldom intrigues or enthralls his interest and his heart. Just as certainly as "the cultivated mind *desiderates a nexus*," so assuredly does a full-blooded personality display an intense and insatiable love of "people." Hence, it seems that the enduring part of literature must be autobiographical, and that abstract things must be seasoned in the stuff of life. And since it is the biographical side of literature which touches most closely the primary fibres of human nature, and gives to thought and events their authentic setting, it would seem evident that its study would greatly help one to envisage and evaluate life.

Then, as over against the study of nature, as well as over against the study of abstract ideas, "the proper study of mankind is man." Not, indeed, would we set in opposition "the wide ocean and the living air," *and* "the mind of man"; but in all appraisements of worth, what is shown as complementary must also be exhibited as subordinate, and the provisional character of nature must be set in the light of the supreme and final value of man. The wind sings its different note under different trees, as it passes through different formations of foliage ; and a blind man can often tell you whether the wind is blowing to him over heather or over the grass, by the subtle difference of sound it makes to his sensitive ears ; but how infinitely more varied are the effects created by the Wind of God as it blows across the spirits of men ! " The sea like a harper lays hand on the shore like a lyre," Swinburne sings ; but in man a more wondrous Harper touches a harp with a thousand strings and brings forth a much more varied and subtle music ! Hills take on a different colour at different times. They may appear grey at sunrise, green at noonday, blue at night, all depending upon the envelope of atmosphere through which the sun pours its rays ; but how very many more varied hues of blue and grey there are in the moods of the human soul ! When Mrs Humphrey Ward went to the hills and lakes of Westmorland as a girl, she said she took those hills and lakes to be " the picture." When later she met Mr Ward and he accompanied her there, she confesses that a change had taken place ; Mr Ward became " the picture " and the hills and lakes became the frame.

And it is the " human document " every time that gives to biography its undying appeal and value. It is the human element, too, which often redeems an otherwise poor specimen of the art. For, be it confessed, some biographies are not worth our pains. " We ought to lose no time in reading them ! " They are like the buses which run " full or empty." Nothing seems to happen in them, but morning, noon and night—only duration, and, on your side, tedium. This is particularly the case when " retirement and reminiscence run in harness together " —though there are great and notable exceptions. Sometimes biographers, too, show little sense of what is vital, and " dole out their pounds in pennies "—of whom, as Coleridge said, " beware." But sometimes in the dreariest pages you get some touch of phrase, some trivial incident which gives as in a flash a view of some rare vein in character. How often you come across " people of whom much more might have been made " —mothers-in-law, step-mothers, maiden aunts, and poor relations who have been as " the angels of God " in some great man's life, and have indeed made possible his work. Great men are not so self-sufficing as they appear from their public performances. No one knows biography, who fails to feel an

enhanced regard for men and women of the lowlier order whose
name stands indissolubly associated with the more conspicuous
people they attended. Who that knows Sir Walter Scott can
forget Will Purdie, his woodsman and gamekeeper? How the
published memories of the various members of the Benson
family, all overflow in appreciations of the wisdom and worth of
" Beth "—for over seventy years the family nurse! Or Maria
Millis in the family of the Shaftesburys! or " Cummy " in the
household of the Stevensons! Who, either, could fail to feel
the friendliest interest in " the gardener," " the baker," " the
cheesemonger," " the postman," or the pedlar who sold 'aporths
o' tea and prayed like a millionaire; rough, rugged, simple
people who met in James Smetham's class at Stoke Newington
and whose features are discernible in the Apostles in his painting
of " The Lord's Supper."

Through his biography a writer you are acquainted with
makes you his " intimate "—or as little Hartley Coleridge put
it, " his *in*quaintance." He stretches " hands across," " gives
himself away," and in doing so " takes you in." By his other
works he perchance has " plucked you by the sleeve," or it may
be " taken you by the collar "—you have the feeling sometimes
that Denney does this—but through his life story or his letters,
and the disclosure of some rough bit of road he travelled, or
some dark shadow that lay across his life, he " pulls at your
heartstrings." Henceforth, you travel together. You may
perhaps be winding your way through the labyrinthine mazes
of Jones' *Philosophy of Lotze* when you pick up that same writer's
Old Memories, and as you take hold of the *man*, you gain touch
with the *philosopher*; you visualise to yourself the stiff uphill
fight he had, to get " from awl to all "; and his " made up "
toggery from the scant wardrobe of his brothers in which he
sat for his examinations, and you " bend your mind one way " to
pursue the thought of a man who has won his title to your regard.
Or engaged in *A Faith that Enquires* the Gifford lecturer seems
to build a pier towards you, and succeeds in making you aware
of the state of his mind about a few things in general and some
things in particular, hailing you across the distance from his side.
But when you read in his Memoir of the heroic fight he was
making with a mortal disease during the whole time he was
writing this work, the *man* builds a bridge right over to your
side and whispers in terms of " a faith that achieves " his profound
reading of man's life and God's purpose in the Universe. And

if one has felt the sweet thrall of a much simpler book, like that of Michael Fairless' *Roadmender*, how much tenderer a spell one feels through the vision the biography affords of a frail and gentle lady suffering from spinal disease writing it propped up in bed overlooking the Sussex Downs, and finishing her book with the manuscript on her chest during the last nine days of life. Roadmender she was indeed ! her view of her suffering was that she was serving the footsteps of her fellows.

Through the study of Journals and Letters, we not infrequently come upon a man's best bits of insight. And who of us has not read truth for the first time in the light which has come to us from other people's windows ? Often the things a man has laboriously prepared, have not the sap of life in them, such as are in the sayings he throws off spontaneously. " No one is ever at his best who is over-conscious of what he is expected to say." The Pope in *The Ring and the Book* tells of standing in Naples and seeing nothing of sea or town or sky, and then, suddenly in a lightning flash he sees all. That is how the great truth of The Living Christ came to Dale. " He lives ! He lives !" he cried as he paced his study. That is how realisation came to James Smetham. " I never come upon a truth at once," he says, " I wake up to it, and then it is utterly real to me." Rabbi Duncan's *Colloquia Peripatetica* is full of such insights. The creative instinct in not a few is quickened, as it was in Aristotle, by walking up and down. One wonders whether it was such " suggestibility " which led both Dr. Maclaren and Dr. Denney to put on their heavy boots when they were finding their preparation going hard, or whether it was, in each, a Scotsman's scorn of ease, and grim set will to master circumstance. To content ourselves with such expressions of truth as one finds in a writer's *magnum opus*, may mean that we miss what is most illuminating as a disclosure of the writer's own mind, and most interpretative of the enigma of his personality. For has not Prof. Gilbert Murray acknowledged that he never knew how much he had missed in Shakespeare till he had read Bradley's pencilled notes in a volume of his he was handling ? And did not Charles Lamb affirm that Coleridge's best insights were in the pencilled notes he made in the books you lent him, such as that which he made once in a book of Thomas Adams' *Private Thoughts* ?—" For a great part of my life I did not know I was a Laodicean, and even after I did discover it I did not feel it aright. I was deceived about my true self, by the sayings of some so-called philosophers, and by some scraps of poor poetry, but most of all by the pride of my poor heart."

" Every man will speak of the Fair according to his market," of course, and the scale in respect of the value of biography will turn for different men at different points. For some, its interpretative quality, as a clue to the unknown X of human personality, will slant the balance. For others, the plus quality, " the more " of inspirational force will appear the superlative thing. There is no need, however, " to divide " over an issue where the terms, though distinct, are not dissociated from each other. Inspiration is a preacher's most constant and urgent need. His greatest peril is " fainting." There are times when like Samuel Rutherford, we would sell all we have " to buy a wind." Who of us cannot appreciate T. R. Glover's saying that often, when he would not give a " thank you " for a counsel, he would give almost everything for an inspiration? What shall we do when " we carry on long debates with despair "? What shall we do to stir and start our souls, when, as Edward Fitzgerald puts it, " all our *go*, such as it was, is *gone* "? Part of the trouble in such hours is that " inertia lies within equality." We live by admiration. Our relief lies in the communion of saints. Is there one of us who has not experienced the tidal wave of some deeper soul lifting him out of his meaner care? There is John Cairns bearing on his heart the shadow of an unrequited love, moving among his fellows with a walk which was a lesson in evangelical humility, he alone unconscious of his greatness. There is Bishop Westcott who read and worked in the spirit in which he prayed, who lived the common life as one who served at the altar, who felt, when he entered the splendours of Auckland Castle, miserable until he discovered a way of making its grounds a public possession; who entered his carriage as if it had been a hearse until he could discover someone to whom he might give a lift. There is Bishop Paget who ever approached his fellows gently, as one bearing flowers. Under the inspiration of such remembrances, one heart, I know, in its dullest moods brightens up like a newly-stirred fire.

Then, this study covers so amazingly wide a field, it is especially fitted to develop catholic sympathies, and to provide the necessary corrective of the narrowness likely to be engendered by specialist activity. Since it is " with all saints " we are to discover the love which passeth knowledge, we do well to set ourselves to the appreciation of different types of piety, and no more helpful sphere than the lives of the saints can be found. We may not be predisposed to the Sacerdotal type, but who can resist George Herbert when he takes up his viol and lute, and beats out the music of the Church's faith and forms in his songs? We may not feel attracted by the vagaries and super- stitions of some of the Mystics, but we can appreciate the religious sensibility of Henry Vaughan, who

> " Feels through all this earthly dress,
> Bright shoots of everlastingness."

" Really good men, the world over, mean very nearly the same thing, though they say many different things, and say many things differently." How fragrant of the true spirit of Christianity is the story told of Cardinal Newman in the life of Dr. Alex Whyte. The Cardinal told the Doctor that he had twelve shrines in his heart, and that recently the occupant of one of them had died. He craved the honour of filling the vacant one with the person of Dr. Whyte. John Morley told his friend, Professor J. H. Morgan, that if Newman had been in Oxford during his time, he believed he would have fallen under his spell. Professor Du Bois said that he made it a point of special care to study that side of life and truth he felt least inclined to. He was always on the watch against the danger of becoming one-sided. His conception of truth was before all else—" the force that makes for unity." Too often, he held, and for too long, we have identified our opinions with the truth itself, and made creeds the instruments of exclusion, rather than as they should be, the articles of testimony. Our action is too often like that of the man who, having seen the light through a chink in his own door, must bring everybody else to see it through that same small chink. Biography has no greater service to render than to teach us to discriminate more clearly between opinion and knowledge.

An initiation into many a branch of knowledge, that is " off our beat," may often be gained along this path. Many, too, who are set upon living life intelligently, but must perforce pursue knowledge irregularly, would find this approach best. The ordinary text-book makes them feel the rein unpleasantly before they get going, and they settle with assiduity rather than avidity to their task. They need to pull down the branch on which the fruit they covet is found, and it so readily springs skywards again. Biography helps to divest knowledge of much of its abstract character ; and through it the writer, instead of stepping athwart our path as he tends to do in the text-book, comes alongside, and we get into step with him. Who that has read Alfred Marshall's *Memoirs*, can fail to be spurred to read his *Principles of Political Economy* ? Fearing lest he should become a mere thinker, he sought to humanise his own sense of the study of Economics. So in his study he kept a small oil painting of a poor man with wistful down-and-out expression. He called him his patron saint. He sought to sense what it felt like to live shadowed with sorrow and shamed with want. It helped him, he said, to keep Economics the servant of practice, and the handmaid of Ethics. It became a corrective when he was tempted to think of the world as made up of tendencies and forces rather than men and women. In the letters, too, which pass between Westcott and Marshall one finds the elements of a real education in the fine points of social justice. Or if Theology is the chosen study, what more helpful initiation could be found, say, than through the lives of Bushnell, Brooks, Dale or Du Bose ? Besides, these could be read in the by-going, or when one was tired. Biography helps greatly, too, to emotionalise ideas and to personalise eras. Fitzgerald held that no more vivid understanding of the 18th century could be gained, than that which was available through *The Journals of Wesley*, *The Letters of Walpole*, and *The Life of Johnson*.

We come in this study, too, upon personality in the making. Charles Reade once expressed regret that it was mostly given to us to see heroes only after their minds had been made up. But biography has its story of a man's wistful waiting, and his struggle with uncertainty, his false starts, his long schooling in disappointment, and his final emergence upon his true career. We get the enthralling record of how men turned necessity to glorious gain, and bore themselves like valiants under the harsh disciplines of " making do " and " doing without." One sees, again and again—as to mention only one case, Goethe : " The flourish drop in the interests of the forming fruit." We view men getting their education for life by any and every kind of way—by humiliation, accepted suffering and sacrifice. " By these things men live "—whilst weaklings die. We see such as Donald Hankey wrestling with that " wretched family failing of not being able to express himself." Men laying in dust life's glory dead, and finding " life that shall endless be." Horace Bushnell and Edward Irving, at not greatly separated times, both losing a son, and both with a strange communion of mind, confessing that the loss of the earthly presence of a son had been richly compensated for in " the revealing of *His Son*, in me." Who does not share, say, the glow of triumph with R. L. Stevenson—of imagination over invalidity—and recount with pleasure how playing at soldiers one damp day in the garden, his nurse threw a shawl over his shoulders, and the reply in scornful tones, " Soldiers don't wear shawls " : then the shawl once more thrown over the same shoulders by loving hands, after being thrown off ; the momentary shadow, and then the thrilling piercing insight, " O, this is not an invalid's shawl, it's a soldier's cloak." Or, who that knows, does not visualise again and again to himself the compact of Henry Jones and his friend, by the side of the little Welsh brook, " By God's help, we'll both get our degree " ; or that other scene, this time two Scots, Andrew Fairbairn and James Strachan, sitting in the back room of James Strachan's mother's house, clasping hands and determining to help each other to study for the ministry ?

Biography, too, is very fruitful in its disclosures of how lives overlap and events converge. It has much to tell of the providential conjunction of personalities. It seemingly was the intention of Robertson Nicoll, who probably knew biographical literature better than any other man, to make some contribution upon this pregnant topic, but the war intervened, and he felt he could not go on with it. He did more than once attempt a kind of genealogical table which read : " Coleridge begat Maurice, and Hort and Maurice begat R. H. Hutton. . . ." The possibilities along that path are endless, and the results of research would be distinctly interesting and valuable. One feels there is no little significance in the conjunction of the '59 Revival with the issue of Darwin's epoch-making book ! How full of fruit for reflection there is in the way in which Berkeley, Butler and Wesley, each set himself along his own line, " to awaken the dormant consciousness of the Eternal Spirit in the religiously slumbering life of the 18th century ! " Sometimes, too, in this kind of study you come upon some notable event, which is variously narrated and named, in some such way as the sea may be differently named as it washes different coasts. It is possible, *e.g.*, to come upon the story of Moody's Cambridge Mission to Students in 1882, in quite a dozen biographical records, and every one has some new phase to emphasise. I notice, for example, that Bishop Moule after telling much the same story as A. C. Benson and Hope Moulton, of the unseemly ragging the students gave the Missioner the first night in the Corn Exchange, proceeds to tell how, on the last night, when a great number rose to profess allegiance to Christ, he, kneeling by Moody as they gave their witness, heard the Missioner say, under his breath, " My God ! this is enough to live for ! " Collocations by the score suggest themselves which cannot be recounted here—two accounts, e.g., of a conversation Wagner and Schumann once had, in which they each reported their impressions ; the remarks say, which Macaulay, Ruskin and Erskine each pass, on the occasion of different visits to the Avre and the Rhone ; the different and yet always deep impressions Forbes Robinson made on his friends by his personality and his letters ; the mark Wilberforce made upon different types of men—and so on.

Just as interesting a record is furnished in the pages of biography, too, of the turning points in the lives of their subjects. There is a biography of crisis as well as a theology of crisis, and it is a most soul-stirring study. Places seem to become indissolubly associated in the mind of the reader, as well as in the experience of the writer, with the particular soul experience which transpired. What Leith Walk meant to Carlyle, the Brig o' Dee largely meant to Rabbi Duncan ; it was a place of soul crisis. Herbert Stead, too, found leaning over Magdalen Bridge at Oxford " the higher certainty." Edward Irving and H. G. C. Macgregor, had alike, such soul-quickening experiences on the Wild Moors as almost inevitably to suggest the lines of Browning, perhaps with a significance never intended by the poet :

> " I crossed a moor with a name of its own,
> And a certain use in the world no doubt ;
> But one hand breadth of it shines alone,
> In the wild waste round about."

After a period of " stumbling over the dark mountains," Elizabeth Fry, H. B. Stowe and R. W. Dale, each in their own way, when listening to the preaching of the Word, came to the crisis of their lives ; the Quakeress, in the Meeting House at Norwich ; Harriet Beecher under " a frame sermon of her father's " at Lichfield ; whilst Dale, listening as a lad to Sherman preach, " suddenly forgot both preacher and audience, as the truth came home to him, that opened for him a new world and a new life." The three "turning points" in the life of Professor W. P. Du Bose are most enthrallingly related and should be read. The stories of how J. R. Illingworth and F. D. Maurice came to a sense of vocation : the first to the conviction, as a boy of seventeen, that he was to interpret the Incarnation so as to correlate the claims of reason and revelation ; and the second, that he was sent into the world to persuade men to recognise Christ as the centre of their fellowship with each other—are records which assuredly are "historic."

And, finally, Biography presents many startling contrasts and echoes many a grave warning. By the time a life story is printed, many a wheel has run round its full circle, and the history of both ideas and men is their judgment. One sees how, say, such a proposition as Robert Owen's that "man's character is made not by him, but for him," works out to its futile end. How, "where Bunyan's statue stands facing where stood his gaol." How Naturalism works itself round to nausea as it did in Holbrook Jackson's "men of the eighteen-nineties." How "the promise of the morning" echoed in the epitaph of a man with spiritual ideals like Kingsley, is contrasted with the mournful "omen of darkness" in the epitaph W. K. Clifford suggested for himself, "I was not, I loved, I am not." One sees how Evangelicalism has been abundantly justified of her children, but also that she has often tragically overlaid some of her noblest offspring by her unmotherly habit of prescribing in too narrow and rigid a fashion the forms in which her children's faith should express itself, and the fixed number of inches of the strait way by which their feet should travel, and so has provoked aversion before she has given her children time to develop appreciation. A veritable Rachel Evangelicalism seems in the 7th, 8th and 9th decades of last century "weeping for children" she never need have lost had she been a wiser and more far-seeing mother. A far different warning issues when one turns from where pressure had been too great to where years of unprotected freedom had been the peril, as many like Coleridge, "an archangel a little damaged," can testify. Perhaps nothing better in the way of striking contrast, and of the raising of sharp issues, has been written on this line than Dr. W. Newton Clarke's small brochure on the life stories of Phillips Brooks and Huxley.

These two biographies raise significant issues, and a word in conclusion, is due to them. All the more so, because they

show traces of those subtle movements of thought, the gradations of which are far too vaguely summarised in history, often
as " changes in the spirit of the age " ; but which, as Professor
A. V. Dicey remarks, it is the distinctive province of biography
to preserve. The lives of these two " dynamic " personalities
cover practically the same transitional period. They met
occasionally, but never established contact. Living on different
continents, they also dwelt in two continents of thought.
Huxley's interest focussed itself on the sub-human world ; he
looked down on his field, and the decisive facts for him were
physical rather than personal. He held, too, that what man
had done, might well be neglected in favour of what man might
do. Brooks, on the other hand, made man central, and set
nature at the circumference. He turned with all his strength
to the study and service of man, and suffused his mind with the
great thoughts of the past, holding that no heritage was ours
which was merely accepted passively. He looked up to his field
in the spiritual life of man, and saw that the problem of man's
soul and of God arise together, and if they are to be solved, must
be solved together. Huxley thought, not in terms of man's
larger freedom, but in terms of nature's structural development ;
and chemical affinities seemed more significant for him than
personal relationships. Limiting himself to such instruments
as his study of nature placed within his hand, Huxley felt that
a personal quality in the administration of the universe was
undemonstrable, and therefore, to him, unacceptable. Thus a
great region of human experience was for him a blank. In this
realm which seemed non-existent to Huxley for want of evidence,
Brooks lived and moved, and had his being, developing a rare
and radiant personality. He struck out in flight into what the
other felt to be a vacuum, and found it to be sustaining air.
Brooks held that the spiritual world is found, not by speculating
about it, but by landing on it, living in it. Huxley would not
admit the existence of any region to which he could not go on
his two feet, or arrive at by the ordered steps of logical sequence.
The two biographies present most sharply the crux of the situation
to-day. Is personality " base born," or has it a birthright ?
Are we, or are we not, to interpret the universe in terms of the
highest it contains   In any full answer to these questions,
biography has not a little evidence to contribute, for along all
its lines the conviction is borne that the spirit of man will never
consent to be choked.